**ANCHOR BOOKS**

FP 2001 SERIES . . .
A SEARCH FOR INSPIRATION

Edited by

Neil Day

First published in Great Britain in 2001 by
ANCHOR BOOKS
Remus House,
Coltsfoot Drive,
Peterborough, PE2 9JX
Telephone (01733) 898102

HB ISBN 1 85930 894 5
SB ISBN 1 85930 899 6

FOREWORD

In today's world, everyone's life is fast-moving and hectic, leaving little time for us to gather our thoughts.

But there are times when we all need to be alone to think things through and sort out our feelings. Many people find poetry is the best way of expressing themselves and helps to reflect on their life.

FP 2001 . . . A Search For Inspiration is an anthology of poetry written by everyday people. They have come together and written down their thoughts and emotions in the form of a poem. The poets have written about many subjects from life and love to places and people. All of the poets have written from the heart, creating a delightful and varied poetry collection.

Neil Day
Editor

CONTENTS

UNTITLED

Victoria, you're like a queen,
a picture in a magazine.
Your hair so fair, your eyes so blue
I love all the things you do.

You're growing up and soon you'll be
a little girl sat on my knee,
and then before we really know,
you won't have much more to grow.

You'll become a woman like your mum
and what a beauty you'll become.
A model or a go-go dancer?
This question only you can answer.

And then one day you'll meet a lad
who'll take the place of your dad
and when he asks, 'Will you be my wife?'
Another man is part of your life.

But I won't worry or be sad
I will only be too glad
to walk with you up the aisle
as long as you are happy and you smile.

And then I'll wait for the day
with another girl I will play.
A granddaughter if I'm lucky
who, like you, will sometimes get mucky.

But all this is a long way off
so stay as you are, a little toff
and on your birthday every year
I'll thank God that you are here.

John Halliwell
(1974)

URCHINEAVEN

It's a long, long walk, in this way of mine, over the moors and streams.
A whole life's journey I cannot decline, drawn back here by
Nature's dreams.
Attracted in youth, perhaps just by chance, lured away from
grimy roads.
The soul was touched by a hint of romance,
My spirit had found new abodes.

The thrill of such space, new worlds to seek out, with no
restraining walls.
Room to tumble and climb, to scream and shout and splash in
ice-cold falls.
The scale so enormous dark mountains so tall, their peaks immersed
in mist.
From one so used to the factory wall,
What wonders had I missed?

Round mournful reproach in a young calf's eyes, caught in its
lonely byre.
The course black tongue dealing shock and surprise, setting the arm
all afire.
Sheep playing tag in the heather and gorse, or trying to stare
you through.
When youth's only companion stray dog or worse,
Sweet enrapture in nature's new zoo.

The breeze from the heather, so scented, so strong, with hair and clothes
blown awry,
Harsh cries of a grouse wafted swiftly along, lost souls calling
to the sky.
Is someone watching, bent on design, in this lonely wondrous vault?
Is it a corner of somewhere, revered, divine?
Do I trespass, am I at fault?

In cold winter months, all muffled white, the moors may appear
to dreams
Streams hidden, invisible, suspended in flight, where silence
reigns supreme.
But life goes on, say the signs in the snow, it's only a seasonal thing.
To love this place dear, accept all its show
Not just beginning with spring.

If this be Heaven, give me more than a taste, to foster this
growing need.
To sample more, let not one minute waste. A life is too short indeed.
This fond plea from a boy, now in a man's place, a prayer time
will not sever.
Please Fate, if barred from Upstairs Grace,
May I stay here, forever?

Erchin Diss

KINGFISHER

Look! A kingfisher, oh where does he go,
When grey winter skies hang sullen with snow,
Does his blue pinions dull and his orange patch fade
As he skims o'er the ice in some barren glade.
And what might he catch when there's ice on the pool,
And he glints 'gainst the snow, like some rare winter jewel,
Does he roost in the hole by the bulrushes clump,
The entrance half-hid by the old water pump.

Is it instinct that tells him when it's time to flee,
To fly to the southward, to some sunlit lea,
To fly to the south, away from the snow,
What is it that tells him that it's time to go,
I know that there's some stay by water's ice-brim,
Looking bedraggled, tattered, and thin,
With feathers unkempt and some rather skewed,
As they swoop o'er the shallows, in their search for food.

But some will survive to see Spring again,
Come wind and come weather, come sunshine and rain.
Winged assegais coated with amethysts, blue,
A sight of great beauty and brilliance of hue.
A flash of pure colour, as he up-river darts,
To lift up one's soul, and gladden one's heart . . .
The king of the river, 'tis springtime he brings,
As blackbird and thrush and the sweet blackcap sings.

John Whittock

PLEASE HELP ME DEAR FRIEND

I don't want to be persistent,
And also be irrisistant.
I just want to go for a walk,
And have a private talk.

I need to talk to someone who I know,
And not have my heart tied up like a bow.
I don't want you to get me in trouble,
And making me burst my bubble.

I need my true friends, to help me with my emotional stress,
And help me get out of my mess.
I really need my true friends to talk to,
And never ever tell me what to do.

Susie Bell

GOODBYE

The time has come, to say goodbye,
The flower has wilted,
Face facts, it's died.
There is no use in hanging on,
Let your life carry on.
Don't let yourself be trampled all over,
Pick yourself up, be strong, don't smoulder.
The pain will fade,
Another flower will grow,
But most importantly,
Your life will go on.

Sumeya Ahmed (13)

DILEMMA

Dear God, a dilemma,
What shall I do?
Whatever I do will be wrong,
So I leave the problem with You.

There's a boy, twenty or so,
Sits on the pavement by the side of the shop.
He looks cold, huddled there in the shadow.
It could be a con, but so what?

I used to always give him a pound.
It eased my shopping therapy guilt,
It wasn't much trouble or effort,
And made me feel cosier all round.

One day, on the way to Waterstones,
He sat in his usual spot.
I went to lay my offering,
But stopped, naively shocked.

He was spaced out,
Drugged, doped, on a trip,
Whatever the in phrase is.
Beyond the world and me.

My money returned to my pocket.
I've never given him anything since.
So there is my dilemma, God.
To give or not? I can't win.

Sheila Wicks

FAITH

Have faith in yourself,
And you can soar like an eagle
So high, yet swooping so low
Over each mountain, each valley.

Your darkest moments
Radiant like the sun.
Your deepest passions
Unveiled and succumbed.

No barrier to restrict
Just freedom
All around,
And beneath it all
A faith that only you can find,
Hidden, waiting to be found.

A life so full so free,
Just smile, a whole new me.
See yourself for who you really are,
Not what others see.

Shine like a rainbow,
Those different colours
Traits in you.
Let that energy, that power,
Burst through.

Elizabeth Childs

THE PARTY

Keep on talking
that's the secret
talking and smiling
the glass raised
to another's bawdy banter
acknowledging the latest gossip
and hoping
these strangers don't sense my strangeness
or that the room which enlivens us
doesn't go back on its word.

Sometimes
a like-minded reveller
will enter my circle
but familiarity breeds fear
like wildfire
and soulmates
seldom speak.

Gary Austin

STAINED-GLASS WINDOWS OF MY DREAMS

A golden thought has just begun
I will make a brave new start today, as if the world was new
As the pretty snowdrops blossom in the sun
And as Mother Nature gets dressed in her splendid colours
And propagates her grass of healing bright green
And puts on her bonnet of blue turquoise sky
For the birds and bees and butterflies to fly on by
The sweet seasons that buds and blooms do bring
And in the sunlight I listen to the red robin sing
Whenever the toils of life are too strong
May the flowing stream in Mother Nature as in life
Make magic changes on earth and all around, astounding
Taste the morning glory fragrance in the scent of spring
A world of joy and wonder as the red robin sings
And where the beech leaves dance and fall
May I look beyond the cares of living and loving
To where the woodland is thriving
Let it be as gold as the morning-glory dew
As if the world had been reborn, anew,
And may it bring love back into my heart and soul
As the aquarian millennium starts to roll
And as my ancient stained-glass windows are open
Come into the colour-therapy of my dreams,
To dry my salty, sadly, lonely tears
As the hurt and pain washed through over the years
May my tears gather dust in a slanted sunbeam
And as I watch the colour of the setting sun
Come on spring, with your golden key
Unlock winter's mystery, show me your tapestry
And all I lack, is a little more time
To look and listen to the robin's rhyme.

Vivianne Hayes

BLACKBIRD

With yellow beak blackbird you bless
The air with myriad note-music mellifluous
Your reveille ransoms sleep and rouses sloth
How lie abed and hear such honorifics
Lauded lightly on the living light of day:
Blackbird warbler, winner of wanton air
Unmaker of melancholia, pillager of misery
Song lift as lightly as the lessening dew
All green grace is by your gift extolled
Your yellow beak and blackened stockings yield
Only to the shaft-lance of the sun through mist seen
No cage could stop the nonce song of your nouns
Even chill of churchyard your trill charms
You shower song of splendour round the spires.

Martin Green

ALONE

The well of darkness surrounds me
As I sink towards coldness and never ending space
My skin becomes liquidised as it flows towards the pit of terror
I reach out to find some comfort as I fall through the eternal
                                                    emptiness of life
Bleeding and bruised I continue my journey of hopelessness
Pushed forward by the invisible force of loneliness and despair.

Joy Meopham

CARPE DIEM

Spring, hesitant unsure through the golden daze of a Monet haze
Summer, verdant, vibrant, lush and bold, a Van Gogh gold.
Autumn, sleep-eyed, drifting down, stubbs russet and brown.
Winter, hoarfrost death, deep-sleep dream, a lowry theme.
Life has its seasons
Its palette of shades
Take note of the colours
Seize the days.

P Naylor

COUNTRYSIDE

Countryside, must never be lost to bulldozer and crane.
Only by planting for the future will their beauty so remain
Old trees, must be replaced, not just chopped down and planed.
Leave homes for the birds, the insects, so each species has food
and light.
To see trees and carpets of bluebells what joy! The gift of sight.

The earth is our future, our food source, our home.
Like the Red Indians, we must respect the earth's bounty if we want
to call it our own.
Let us return to nature and realise that her treasures must be shared.
To show future generations that, this one, really cared.

C Stocks

GENTLEMAN OF THE ROAD

When people see me
Walking down the street,
They say here he comes
An out of work bum,
But I can't help the way I am,
A hobo's my name,
The hedgerow's my home.

I am a gentleman of the road,
I hope I am when I grow old,
Cos this is the only life for me,
Wondering wild and walking free,
I know every hotel dustbin,
I know every park sideseat,
I know all the little children
They're the only ones who speak.

When walking down a country lane,
The birds are my friends,
They sing out my name,
When I'm in the town, it's not the same,
It's not like the lanes,
It's nosy and plain.

The country lanes are the life for me,
The flowers, the trees, playing in the breeze,
There's no one there to tell me to move on,
I go as I please, I might be the breeze
But I'm free,
I'm the gentleman of the road.

Wendy Daisley

SHREWSBURY ABBEY
(for Wilfred Owen)

A spirit roams the timeworn marches,
Tonight it hugs the Shropshire Hills,
Descending on Caer Caradoc
And sweeping Long Mynd's Carding Mill;

Easing down the Severn plain,
Encircling spires and ancient stacks
It slingshots round the river's loop,
'Cross English Bridge for sacred tracts.

Abbey brickwork folds like winds
Of First World War puttees and boots;
Exposed by smoky, yellow lights,
Like haunting flares and grass shell hoots?

Tonight there hangs a moonless sky
But pin-pierced deepness shines its ice,
On crippled trees that blindly guard
The chill death-orchard sacrifice;

Translucent in the silken light,
A granite shrine to a lifetime's end,
A simple message on its side:
'I am the enemy you killed, my friend.'

Philip Huckle

POST

Aftermath
And all is quiet.
Chilled by the silent glow
Of your sleeping moon.
I sobbed, desolate
And my body shook
With the gust
Of a thousand dying stars.
I got up
And sat by the bath
I saw myself
Haunted porcelain
And I knew then
My war is over
Sound the bells.

Freya Pugsley

THE SEA OF GALILEE

Your darkness floats into a ragged horizon,
Tangled hair wreathing a lake
Lying so still the night-air has stopped breathing.
Silent seaweed-currents straggle to unite
Into a loose knot resting at the nape of your neck,
Your past, your tentative present, your future.

Now, now locks loosen, break free and are spreading,
Threading through the orange beads of a distant horizon.
Lights weaving their narrative along your familiar
Coast-line, winding further, upwards upon the forehead
Of the parchment hills of the Golan Heights

Where the dry winds wait for you, the shepherd
To defy the rusting barbed wire criss-crossing the land,
Fencing in our dreams, our hearts which long
To whisper with the leaves of the silvering trees
Peace, yes, now, at last, your long-loved peace.

Heather Lawton

FAIRY STEPS

You put eternity into the hearts of men,
And I've carried it here forever,
Beneath my shirt; come listen.

Come closer
Venture into the deeper pools
Of aching, restless, spiral gaps
Whistling cold through dental cavity.

You lose your head down here;
But it's warm and safe once you're in.
Before you try to fathom again edgy shapes
And find your eyes closed with sticky glue,
No, not closed, not even connected
To make sense of such things, distracted as they are
By property prices and new ways of cooking rice.

But straining in the dark you say;
Look there, further back, there's you -
Dancing in the belly of the last great whale,
Wondering if one chemical reaction
Is more valuable than the next.

And though you cannot begin to see
What God has done from start to stop
(Are you, my guide, still there?)
You see how far you've come
And turning, take another
Cautious fairy step into the dark.

Andrew Pont

JUST FOR NOW

To be near you, in your room
a chair, a sock, a picture, the mirror,
looking at you, looking at yourself
you're not noticing I am there, so what's the change, but
I am happy here just for now.

To be there in your daily life, the bus,
the train, the classroom, watching you think, wondering
what's going on in your mind, but to get closer it's too soon
I can be happy here just for now.

To be there on the other side, the club, the floor,
adrenaline pumping, alcohol running, but somehow
I can get closer now, even kiss sometimes more
but in the aftermath, it's all forgotten, can I be happy here
just
for now.

To be there, without the worry, the anxiety, the want
of just like before
I can't be
But dare I tell you that just for now I want
the feeling of so much more.

Barry McIlhinney

I LIE HERE PEACEFUL

I lie here peaceful in your bed,
Sensing your warm body with mine.
The velvet magic of the night
Is silent music, love's divine.
I feel your touch so soothe my form,
Caressing and exploring every curve.
I feign sleep, and warmth inside me grow,
Flesh on flesh, yet light and new.

I catch you in my deep embrace
And watch your eyes betray your thoughts;
Delight and wonder dancing there,
As you enfold me in your arms.

Then I awake, and dream is broken -
The world is alone now here once more;
Daylight seems a harsh companion,
Yet memory of night remains.

We seem so strong unwavering
Untouchable by the world, but yet
One life is always better shared
No fortress stands on self alone.
God give me back my freedom,
The sanctuary I crave,
We need love now as always;
From cradle-bed to grave.

Nadya James

WAITING FOR MILLI

Puffballed, a marathon run
Like beating wings inside a drum.
Acrobats I'm told you make,
a moon
blown flower,
strewn arms
and legs,
Touchdailed sensitive.
Asleep.
Awake.
Crusted inside your jelly egg,
Watery skirts between us hold,
Shuttled in your fleshy folds.

Shelly Morgan

AFTERWARDS

('He hears it not now, but used to notice such things.' Thomas Hardy)

Green melancholic man, verdigrised with age,
Entombed in bronze, sited at the Town's head.
The sun rises and sets you - motionless.

No more to see the narrowed lanes, cow-caked,
That wend the harvesting fields
And rise atop the high-browed hills
Where once you walked.
No more to tend the sad sparrows in the snow
Nor keep company with Shiremen in the fold.
No more to hear the milkchurns' ladling call;
Or see the Waggoner's upraised greeting hand.
And though you hear not now the thrush
Deep-throated from a bough
Sing out the evening's swell;
Nor do you hear the pylon's marching steel,
Or feel the fume-stacked soot upon your brow.

Time sets you motionless,
Turned towards the west.
Rest in peace Old Man,
You did not pass unnoticed.

Janine Vallor

IN THE JUNGLE

In the jungle, the mighty jungle, the lion sleeps tonight,
wake him up by singing too loud, you're sure to have a fright.
You begin to sway, and move your body to the beat,
he struts over, proud, he's going to sweep you off your feet,
he thinks tonight you'll be his treat.

Another beer, another leer, he makes eye contact with you,
the music gets faster, the smoke screen thickens,
you make your escape to the loo.
Full of girls crying, they were the lion's last conquest,
pouting lips, make-up applied, you try to look your best.
There are unwritten rules, you see,
to catch your king, you must be more pretty,
a better dancer, wear less than all the rest.

Emerge ready for the gauntlet ahead,
the dangerous path to the bar.
One crossed look, one spilt drink, the animals will want you dead.
The panther waits to make his move
as soon as he spots a gap,
the thirsty grow restless, a cheeky monkey
pushes in, he's sure to receive a smack.

You laugh and jig and giggle,
like hyenas in the heat of the night.
The tiger protects the female by his side
from the snake who looks for a fight.

The gorilla on the door keeps watch,
he's there if any trouble arises.
If you enter the jungle hoping for a quiet time
you're in for a few surprises!

Tracy Leyshon

ROSE

Which is the prettiest flower that grows?
Most people say, 'It's got to be a rose.'
With its soft silky petals,
And its green velvet leaves,
And its tall spiky stem,
That sways in the breeze.

It has a sweet-perfumed smell,
That floats softly through the air,
Whenever you feel it,
You feel all fresh and fair.

Elizabeth Anne Holt (11)

THE STATE OF THE NATION

Hopscotch and skipping ropes
things kids play before they get old
Darts and dominoes and lager louts,
financial worries, bread and butter doubts.

Walking the streets for inspiration
chemical warfare and radiation
People begging on the streets
no job, no luxuries, no tasty treats.

Fashion victims and punk rocks
slaughtered seals, suicide whales and polluted docks
don't tell me it's getting better every day
Tibet, Northern Ireland and Tianneman Square
won't go away.
I hate apathy, and the word 'democracy'
some eat off silver plates
while others look forward to their release dates

Kingston Town, a free state,
freedom of speech, not another debate.

George Norris

THOUGHTS

Thoughts to have
Things to say.
Sometimes the thoughts you have are trouble,
And are best kept tucked away.

Tracy Rudman

SMOKE UNTIL YOU CHOKE

Smoke until you choke
It's the in-thing to do
We have all heard of bulimia
But what about emphysema?

Smoke until you choke
Your lungs can take it
You're in your twenties
Run for the bus you'll make it

Smoke until you choke
At forty the cough's naughty
But it's cleared by midday
So that makes it OK

Smoke until you choke
No sign of a stroke
You're in your fifties
But not quite as nifty

Smoke until you choke
You've now had the stroke
The sixties have come without a care
But you're now paralysed in a wheelchair

Smoke until you choke
You're completely broke
Everybody just passing you by
And there you are wanting to die

Smoke until you choke
It's no longer a joke
Throat audibly rasping
And you completely gasping

Smoke until you choke
You can now only croak
You may have enjoyed another five years
Of sipping the occasional beers

Smoke until you choke
Advance to snorting coke
Do you want quality of life? - Well it's your choice
At seventy broke, incontinent and no voice

Smoke until you choke
Now's the time you woke
And at the tender age of fifteen
Growing up not *old* should be your dream

Denise Mather

KIROTAHI

The sun was high
As then the pom arrived.
It was time to ride
Off to the beach we stride.
For a ride on a husaberg.
Husaberg? Or husa-birk!
As the westerly winds blew by,
So the pom flew high
Dried leaves tumble
The husaberg began to rumble
Tumble, tumble went the pom
And oh what a tumble
Cartwheels, broken wheels.
Hop skip and a jump
A hip with a bump
So the pom was dumped
We cruised as the pom was bruised
So was the news
Of how the pom got his bruise.

Grant Kinnaird

HIGH AND LOW

Here sits a man upon a seat
With tired aching and weary feet;
Here comes a woman with a bowl of water
Not too cold; not too hot. Just at the right heat;
With it she had provided a towel and soap
For a better woman he could not hope;
But when he had soaked and dried his feet
There was no sign of this woman he thought so sweet;
He looked high and low for her everywhere
Every avenue and every street;
He could not understand it
Last time he saw her she was in her stockinged feet;
She had disappeared like a mist
And the chap did not like this awful twist,
He kept searching throughout his life
For he wanted to make her his wife;
After some time had gone by
Someone in the crowd caught his eye;
He thought to himself my oh my! It cannot be
I have finally found the woman for me
Approaching with great fear and dread
But hope that it would be friendly what she said;
She was glad to see him and told him so
And that through life with him she wanted to go;
So a short while after they were wed
And both now happy share the marriage bed.

S Glover

DYING TODAY

Bring me my rifle
I need it once more
another war's looming
just outside my door
and if I had the bottle
I'd run far away
but I'll do all my dying
Today

I'll stand and be counted
like the hero once said
I'll duck all the bullets
while he's tucked up in bed
and I'll bury my comrades
as they all drop dead
yes we'll do all our dying
Today

Oh God bless the hero
who sent us to war
who'll give us all medals
like he did once before
oh God bless the hero
I hope he keeps well
as we do all his dying
today down in
            Hell

John Richards

LOVES OF MY LIFE

Sun on my back, rain on my face
Slippers warming by the fireplace
A walk on the beach on a summer's day
With a pot of tea to take away
Siamese cats and pygmy goats
Baby lambs with fleecy coats
Turkish Delight, lemon meringue pie
These are the things that make me sigh
Porridge for breakfast
Crumpets for tea
These are the things that satisfy me

The delicious smell of fresh baked bread
Sleeping children in a feather bed
Looking happy and well-fed
Butterflies and birds in flight
Twinkling stars on a cloudless night
These things give me great delight
Sparkling sea and skies so blue
Trees and flowers of every hue
A cashmere shawl, a velvet coat
These are the things that make me gloat.

Sue Wooldridge

WHERE WILL I BE?

The other night I had a dream
I wonder how the world will seem
In 10 years time where will I be?
Will Grandad still be there for me?

Will Grandad still be in his flat
And will he still have *Sox* the cat?
Still looking through the mags for nags
And smoking those disgusting fags?

Will Arlene still be writing rhymes
And will they bring her happy times
And will she still like Phil the Greek
We think she has a blooming cheek!

Will my dad just stand and stare
And will my mum still do my hair?
Will my dad still use his internet brain
And will my mum have gone insane?

Will we still have Ali cat
And will she still be on our mat?
Will she still be climbing walls
And will she still be mad at balls?

Will my brother still like Rangers
And will he still be shy with strangers?
Will he still transmogrify
Just everything that meets the eye?

Will all these things be happening
When I am famous and I can sing!

Hayley Oldfield (10)

SECRETS AND LIES

You are hiding something from me
Every time I look at you I see it in your eyes
A lie
And every day you say you have nothing to tell
I pull away a little further
Put distance between us
And try and wrench my heartstrings back
To limit the pain
My heart is beating its retreat
Soon, without a whisper, I'll be gone
Your lies will not be able to touch me
And our love will disappear
Drowned in my tears.

A M Houghton

THE SPIDER PLANT

Like lava spilling out of a volcano.
A jungle of curving alligator scales.
Swinging vine, waiting to feed you into
                        the mouth of a beast
The skinny legs of a red-eyed spider.
An old breaking heart ready to pass away.
Hair of an ancient, stranded palm tree.
The blades fight like a hurricane.
Like an army of dying, hungry people.
A beard never shaved, tangled and knotty.
Snakes on the evil head of Medusa.

Leanne Butterworth (11)

MISS YOU

The sky and the sea never seemed so blue,
But all they did, was remind me of you.
The colour in your cheeks,
The wind in your hair,
And all I could think of - was that you weren't there.

Paul J Gee

OPEN OUR EYES

As we immerse ourselves in life,

Selfishly pushing for personal aims,
Oblivious to neighbours' grief and strife.
Let us open our eyes and see

Possessions and power are all we seek,
Since time began, we have argued and fought,
At the expense of others, especially the weak.
Let us open our eyes and see

Genocide, anger, famine and war,
Babies' gaunt faces, hands reaching out,
May we care for them, cry for them, give them more,
Let us open our eyes and see

Peace, hope, friendship and sharing,
A touch, a smile, a greeting,
These are all we need for caring.
Let us open our eyes and see

Think of love and life, love and life is hope,
Join our hands and cradle the world,
Swaddled together, perhaps we could cope.
Let us open our eyes and see

Christ and Lennon spoke of peace, and loving one another,
May race and creed start to live as one,
Forgiving and nurturing each other,
We need to open our eyes and see.

Carol Davis

A Reflection Of The Truth

As I look into a dusty mirror
I see a girl whom I don't know anymore
She has weary eyes as though she's seen so much
For you she hopes it won't happen again, but knows it will.
I turn to a smoke-filled room
With a man in the corner
He is old with a pipe filled to the brim
But my father is only a presence to me.
Out of the window onto the street
There is a storm brewing, sent from the ocean.
The street lights gleam through a sudden mist
A man knifing women like a cat on mouse.
Through a neighbour's open curtains a child
A child sobbing out of fear
As he clutches his toy train
His nanny points a gun to his head.
I hear shrieks of pain from the next room
My sister frightened and trapped
With a strike of the belt
Her killer smiles and kicks her.
Then my best friend knocked upon my door
She didn't need to say a word, I already knew
As the blood ran down, her face seemed to say
'I am black, they are white.'
I turn back to the mirror
This reflection is staring back at me
She has more memories she prays will not be recalled
This woman could be anyone, you or me.

Alice Watson (12)

A TOAST

A toast to all the women who
Were damaged by misuse;
Yet have beaten the oppressor and
Withdrawn from his abuse.
To all the distraught women who
Once hung their heads in shame:
Believed themselves unworthy and
Deserving of the blame.

A toast to all the women who
Ensured the troubled child
Could glimpse the rays of sunshine, hid
Within the darkened skies.
To all protective women who,
Through eyes that shone with tears,
Could smile and reassure the young:
Alleviate their fears.

A toast to all the women who,
Amid their pain and grief,
Clung tightly to their sanity,
Their principles, and faith.
To all courageous women who,
In order to expose
The perpetrator's loathsome acts,
Laid bare their broken souls.

So, here's to all the women who
Have battled to survive.
Please, raise your glass and wish them all
A brighter, future life!

Sandra Wolfe

THE SILENT PARTNER

Go on, hit me,
It's your only response.
Don't get me wrong,
You do it very well.
No one else knows.

No need for excuses.
I was wrong,
I asked for it.
I moved too fast,
Dislodged a speck of dust
You wanted to keep in place.

You think you can beat me,
But I will win.
My day will come,
I'll tell everyone
How I snapped under pressure,
At the end of my tether,
When they find both of us,
You dead, me innocent.

Colin Grimley

HOPES AND DREAMS

I've tried and tried oh, how I've tried
A prize or two to win,
Every day the numbers come
In the daily paper
But, my numbers do not coincide
Not one of them a winner.

I'll try the Christmas wish think I,
We'll see if that's a winner;
My car needs changing really bad,
The house needs decorating;
The central heating bill is high
Needs a change of radiating
The windows let a huge draught in
They really need double glazing.

Should I win a nice big prize
I'd know these things would be done quick
But on top of that I'd want to give;
To some children who need saving,
Their lot is far worse than mine,
And I'd love to help which would be caring and sharing.

There are so many things I would do
If a good prize I could win,
My bingo card I do each day
But, lots of numbers hidden stay;
I'm not saying I want a million;
Just fifty thou' or even half
Would really be quite nice.

I would help the children
Plus some other worthy cause;
My debts I'd clear and change my car,
And when I've done all that,
I'd buy my children and theirs too
A humper-bumper Christmas.

All these things I could do,
And then I'd do much more;
If only a prize win
Would drop through my door.

F J Smith

SILENT SHOUTS

Old man sits in chair,
Holds the hand of boy,
Patiently, with such care
One has learned a lot,
The other a lot to learn.

Aged sad weary and worn
Much knowledge to impart,
Youth sat beside him there,
Each envied what the other had
And he had not.

If age had but youth
If youth were sagacious,
If together they could make one
If, if, if, the thought it burned
Flickering sparks infused both crowded heart.

Not one word spoken
The span of life between too great,
Thoughts, unknown the same
Disallowed to communicate,
Silence speak! No, stay silent sound
Else sweet illusions break.

Diana M Annely

RETURN FROM EXILE

The voices of my friends had often warned me
'Never try to return to childhood scenes.
The changes wrought by war spoil all illusions,
And all your happy memories will be gone.'
But longing for what had been, grew too strong.

So there I stood by what had once been home,
Now just a ruin, with the roof all gone,
The remnants of a door on broken hinges,
Dark holes instead of gleaming, curtained windows,
And all surrounded by a weedy throng.

But then a splash of colour caught my eye
Behind the shelter of a broken porch,
The blooms of tiger lilies reaching for the sky,
Their golden trumpets shining like a flaming torch!
They had withstood the onslaught all along!

These were the flowers I had loved the most!
They had been there, when at my First Communion,
Dressed like a bride, I had received the sacred Host.
When for a little girl the praise of the Almighty
Had been a simple act of faith so strong.

These flowers now restored the pictures in my mind.
They stood as witness that my memories were right.
Life had been colourful, and good and kind
In those days long ago, among my loving people.
But coming back to face the past had not been wrong!

The devastation war and time had wrought
Now fills my heart with thanks for present blessings.
They seem more precious now than I had ever thought.
The beauty, love and friendships of my new abode,
Have made a happy home to which I now belong.

Christel Symon

PUB

Lucky horseshoes?
A gypsy at my table.
Trumpet ears
And rocky noses
And quiet, blue window minds.

Las Vegas in the corner
And Coca Cola dreams.
My swan light,
My milky orange night,
Absent lootly mad.

See the see?

Smoking smokables.
Travelling flavours.
Red heart,
Pure White Hart.
Dirty old men need love too.

Rosie Dee

ROAD RAGE

He glanced at you,
(through rear view)
you,
who are oblivious.
Constant speed,
(about fifty - probably)
perfect mimicry.
More flirtatious motions
wide-eyed disbelief
mating call of . . .
horn,
indicates flashing,
(arrow, amber, that is)
round in circles
glaring off on
a tangent
(growls to pause)
sudden awareness,
defensive stance
but expression of . . .
(fumbling with lock)
innocence.
Condemning voice . . .
ignorance and need
to listen,
(stop, look and)
learn.

Lesley Naul

MY TREE

What is a tree?
A thing of beauty I see
With leaves of green and willowy sheen
And then of Autumn gold and brown, and red
And standing tall.
When all leaves are gone, with nothing on, or rather
This beauty can stop the sun from shining
Can block my daylight, my paths are darkening,
Shadows are lurking, feelings are foreboding, but never
Moving away, my Friend.
But, under its cover in shelter from shower, I stand,
Its spreading hands protect me,
Then at its feet, take rest from the heat of day
Front me a haven from danger or care.
With passing time, my Tree, will no longer be there.

Elen Tai

BLOOD-RED ROSE
(I love you Debbie)

You're a blood-red rose
You've got snow-white icing
on your frozen toes
Got a silver tongue
and electric clothes
and I'm the one-man line at the neon sign
that says you're mine.
I've got a kitten mind, I'll scratch at any movement
that I find
But when you're close to me I'm still and blind
to anything but you.
I use all my charms to sleep in your arms
You're a blood-red rose, breathe your gentle scent
to my bending nose, let me look inside
the stamen grows and when your petals close
around me so, rivers flow.

Jon O'Neill

STOP IT!

It hurts,
A smack,
A sharp, short whack,
But the marks
On skin,
Are nothing
To within.

Kay Heywood

THE FIRE

O' what fun we had with a fire,
Making flames go higher and higher.
Burning things that are no good,
Boxes, paper, lumps of wood.
Baskets, slippers, old car tyres,
Things that people throw on fires.
O' what fun we've had today,
How I wish that I could stay.
'Tea is ready,' Mother shouts,
But I wanted to stay till
              the fire went out.

W Culshaw

RED LIGHT

I went through a red light today.
Brake, clutch, neutral, handbrake,
text-book progression to stop.
Steroid spots, histamine hots.
Bubble pack down to one,
take one a day. Come back
if you don't feel right.
Chemically alive and driving
through a red light.
Artist's eyes, retinally surprised
in detachment, challenged by
fly-shaped hairlines.
Yellow in parallel pairs,
denying resting, testing in code
for the big highway.
I had not done this before.
I had not done that either.
Stopped for breath,
smelling death in all directions.
I went through my red light today.
Green, amber, stop.

John D Burgoyne

THE NAME OF THE ROSE

By what other is she known,
To whose charms, were drawn.
Standing out above the rest,
Could it be the end of the quest?
Always bright, and colourful of kind,
One with such bloom is hard to find.
Has the search come to a close,
Is she the perfect Rose?

Standing proud and strong,
Blooming ever long.
Filling us with laughter and delight,
Giving strength in our plight.
With pride of place on display,
Taken too soon away.
Leaves withering, and petals falling,
With courage, faced the final calling.

Still gracing, with summer's sweet scent,
Of memories in the garden spent.
Without you the darker days loom,
With your grace we lift above the gloom.
To go on you have given cause,
But what is the name of the Rose?
By what other is she known
To whose charms, were drawn.
Standing out above the rest,
My colourful Rose, you are the best.

R Peters

HOMEWARD BOUND FROM EAST CARLTON PARK

Drifts of snowdrops spread
beneath gnarled, aged trees;
a fat robin sitting
in a dense, prickly hawthorn bush.

A tall, stretching church tower
gleaming white in the wintry sun;
a pair of horses, sleek and shiny
out for a brisk morning canter.

Shrieking seagulls sighted massed
and fluttering in flooded fields;
and a warm, wonderful feeling
all is well in my cosy, little world.

Anne E Rutherford

NATURE'S WILL

Oh wind whistling noisily through the lane,
Will you disappear or come back again?
Will you shout or will you groan?
Will you whisper or will you moan?
Will you feel icy-cold or will you be warm?
Will you blow the bees away when they swarm?
Will you blow in March as you usually do
And will you blow bubbles with the morning dew?
Will you whip frenziedly over hills and dales,
Or talk to the animals quietly in the vales?
Will you blow the dark clouds far away
And let the sun shine throughout the day?
When you are angry will you blow buildings down
Or just pass noisily from town to town?
Will you make the mighty ocean roar
Or will you let peace reign for a little while more?
We may not want you but we need your power
So we need your energy every available hour,
The flour mill and the ships on the ocean too,
All depend on the benevolence of you.

S Ball

LIFE'S FORGOTTEN FEW

Whilst walking down a street
A tramp and a wino you chance to meet
Do you ignore them as you pass by
Or say to yourself I wonder why?

Now that is a question to make you think
Why the tramp took to the road, the wino to drink
Did the tramp suffer heartbreak sometime in life
Maybe the loss of a much-loved wife?

And what of the wino, what sort of strife
Turned him to drink and ruined his life?
Was it no work, a wife and kids to support
He stole for them and felt so ashamed when caught?

Now they go their own way, their burdens to bear
And we never seek reasons because we don't care
Is it because the gods smiled down on us
That we just walk by and don't give a cuss?

So just say to yourself as you walk by
It's only by the grace of God on high
                            There go I.

W Parham

BY THE CAMPFIRE

Ahhh! What a great place to be,
Beside our bold fire.
Passionate flames that climb higher and higher.
With its shimmering glow
You can hear the wood sigh.
We sit and we watch as time passes by.

As time passes by, it's just me and you
Enjoying the quiet and wonderful view.
An abundance of stars strewn out round the sky,
Like glitter on velvet.
We watch and we lie.

As we lie by the fire, in silence, we listen
Waves lap onto shore, you can see the loch glisten,
We lay our heads down and our eyes start to tire.
It's so peaceful . . . by the campfire.

Roseanne McCafferty

MY NAN IS *GREAT!*

My Nan is great.
She is my mate.
She's never late.

She is *So* great.
In Nan's old *red* car
We do go *f a r . . . r . . . r*
To town
       And around
           And we do hang around.
Nan is getting a new car . . .
Hope we still go far.

It's getting late.

Thomas Wilkins (7)

MAPLE SKY

I woke up late this Monday morning,
to another mundane day just like before.
I thought I saw that I was happy,
but I know that smile is yours.
As I wait impatiently,
on a rainy day again.
Don't you crave my company,
now that I'm just called a friend?

I thought I heard you call my name,
but the voice was in my head.
And I'm to blame for all your sadness,
I didn't mean to make you mad.
I thought I saw your pretty face,
just once in another's eyes.
And there I thought I kissed your lips,
underneath a maple sky.

Daniel J Horsman

A VICTIM'S WORD I

10-2, *Not guilty!* Why?
Only you did tell the biggest lie.

Justice supported you
Justice left us bare
Away from the courtroom
Without a child's care.

Free to go, to carry on,
Free to do another child wrong.

Haunted memories linger still.
Forgive Law's jury - we never will.

10-2, *Not guilty!* Why?
       Only God has heard your wicked lie!

D Gabriel

ALL IS WELL

The crescent moon, so beautiful, so tender in the sky,
The hills and valleys stretching out, the birds and bees, they fly
And night comes soon upon the land, the clouds and shadows grey,
And magic fills each night, each dawn, until the next bright day.
Rain it pours upon the roof and cattle sit and low,
And all is peace and winter's bliss, within the fire's glow.
The sunset haze so beautiful so tranquil, scenes of blue
The Golden Light of love and rest, moves over each anew
And life is fresh and young and true, the way it's always been
And many men will take their hands and move into the green
And then there's love and stealthy girls that look so sleek, so fine
And people who you never knew upon the distant mine
And melodies of symphonies are playing out so loud
You disappear beneath the sun and mingle in the crowd.

Pamela Coope

A Lost Stubbs' Painting Found!

The painting's British owner was unaware
That it was mentioned yet not shown, in books on Stubbs.
After cleaning, the artist's signature emerged . . .
The horse, 'Euston', stood there with his jockey - joy surged
Through all who looked at him. He would cause some hubbubs.

In the academic, and art worlds, he's been found
In his dapple-grey glory; with rider in red
Racing colours, he stands in a spring river scene.
Without loss in eight meeting starts, his form was keen.
Seldom had such a noble strong-eyed horse been bred.

Gillian C Fisher

THE HUNT

I run,
The hunt sounds loud behind me,
The dogs bay,
Howling the death song,
I run,
The horn sounds,
The horses gallop on my tail,
I run,
Through magical glades,
The birds are silent,
The hunt has been death to so many,
The stream looms,
I jump,
I'm free,
The song of the hunt has gone!
Freedom!
I run,
I jump,
This time,
For joy,
For I am free,
I will live,
To see a new day,
In the leafy glade,
That's home.

Anne Hayes (13)

COBRA

Cobra, cobra, on the ground,
Biting everyone around,
People running for their lives,
As the powerful creature dives.

It strikes with crushing jaws,
It doesn't know the laws,
So it thinks it's the king,
Of course the king of his ring.

Cobras burn with brightness,
It doesn't care the slightest,
Its jaws are strong as iron,
Its fangs can kill lions.

Cobras can be cannibals,
Cobras can be animals,
Humans need knife blades,
So life does not fade.

Cobra, cobra, on the ground,
Biting everyone around,
People running for their lives,
As the powerful creature dives.

Thomas Fox (9)

BEING AN INDIVIDUAL

I would hate to live in the 50s

Because the Blacks were not recognised as individuals.
There is too much war and little love

Soaps are just as bad
You show me a person off Coronation Street
I will show you a transvestite
He has to wear trousers in public and skirts in his own room

If you speak up for a person excluded from a group of friends -
Then you too are different
If a black man wants to join the police, he is a traitor
A famous man spoke out for his own race -
Martin Luther King -
And was brutally murdered.

We've all done things we are ashamed of

Heaven is my perfect place - everyone is someone
Here is a question
Would you respect me if I had a gun?

Paula Renee Morgan

SUCCESS

Don't waste away
Live life to the full each day
Get out of bed and comb your hair
Try to act as if you even care
Success
Take a walk and clear your head
Don't spend all day in bed
You can be anything you want
A DJ or a vagabond
Success
Hopes and dreams really do come true
This is why I'm talking to you
Loneliness is hard to face
If you let it,
It will take your place
It's up to you to find your way
Don't stay alone today
Go out and find somebody who
Will share your hopes and dreams with you
Success
The world is your oyster
So make up your mind
To do it now or wait till next time
It doesn't matter who you are
You could be the next superstar.
Success.

Margaret Doran

BEHIND CLOSED EYES

Listen,
Can I hear Trelawney's men
As they marched in years gone by?
Did I hear a thousand voices sing
Of a white rose and a rugged cross
And the 'Merry Maidens' Ring'?

And was my heart not filled
With longing for the past?
I see yet still the roughness
Of the bracken-covered moors.
I hear yet still the boiling seas
Washing smooth the Cornish shores.

Will my heart not miss old 'Davey'
With his lantern held so high?
And the ghosts of bygone miners
With hollow footsteps passing by.
And of those that heard the rumblings and the
                                    tremors of the Earth
The tin ore graves, the helpless sighs
The land that saw my birth?

And in my rest of darkened silence
Behind closed, eyes, throughout the night,
A million memories race, in colours
Bringing pain and happiness
And putting right my mental plight.
Relieving all that's gone before.
Kindling and keeping alive my sightless treasures
Enticing desire to relive it once more.

Sue Smith

TIME

If we could unlock the secrets
Of the past, present or to come,
What knowledge could be revealed,
What power would be obtained,
But time cannot be suppressed
That immeasurable expanse of eternity
Surpassing all that man is, knows and has.

Sharon Ferguson

WHY?

The day he left her I cried and cried.
The day he no longer wanted her as a wife.
The one I adored, I trusted and loved
Had betrayed his family, my father it was.
He left us all feeling numb with pain
That things would never be the same again.
There was nothing we could do to make her feel better -
Just make cups of tea which now seems pathetic.
Two years have passed and what has he gained?
He says he is happy, but he's not the same.
Mum is strong now and has got a life
But I think she still misses being his wife.

Sarah Jane Pinkett

ANCIENT SOUND

Honeyed summer days, bees of barbed sting eager
seeking sweet taste, dusty pollen, yellow coating
tiny feet, tiny knees, ever-whirring wings.
The sound of buzzing, more ancient than the rolling
hill, sharp brambled lanes, or cultivated plots, where
varied flowers grow.
Older, older than the hand, that sure guides the plough
or the choir voices, some off key, that mournful sing,
or church bells of smelted copper, tin, that joyful ring.
Little insects soldier on, empires slowly rise, prosper,
stutter, swiftly fall.
And all the while, Old Father Time, hypnotic ticking,
tocking, from within long clock, standing tight against
the wall.

He loves long sunny days, overflowing honeycombs,
dislikes idleness, misty rain, hidden webs, sudden cold.
More precious than the rarest gem, exotic-scented myrrh,
or heavy pure gold.
The humble bee, a tiny spark of Nature's soul.

W W Thomas

SHH!

Shh! I'm watching a film
Shh! I'm listening to the radio,
Shh! I'm reading a book.

Shh! I'm waiting for a phone call,
Shh! I'm reading the paper,
Shh! I'm driving my car.

Shh! I'm playing on the computer,
Shh! I'm trying to sleep,
Shh! I'm mowing the lawn.

J Bishop

STILLBIRTH

Beyond the polished gold,
Beyond what you know
-          there is me,
A foetal shadow.

Can't you see me screaming?
My toothless wailing burns my eyes
-          passes over your ears.

Just leave me alone,
Leave me to look at the stars,
I don't want your help,
your company,
your condolences
-          your changes.

You've never seen my face,
My wide lifeless eyes, windows to my depravity.

Pick me up,
Hold me close to your chest,
Support my little head.

But my chubby fingers can't grasp,
I fall and sever my spine.

Motionless like marble,
I'm numb now,
I don't think,
Neither do you,

We just ignore.

Laura Holt

72

SPRING DAY

Curlews cry over the waiting moor
A clear bubbling cry that stirs the heart
That thrills through the breeze
Rippling the bog grass
In silky undulations
Already the brown desolation of winter
Is shredding away
And the moor smiles under a renewing sun
Would that the icy bleakness of my winter
Could so dissolve and this same spring
Warm into life my frozen spirit
Agonised I cry into the wind
Am I alone winter-dead
Captive in the Snow Queen's kingdom?
Through the tangy air
Come answering voices
Wind whispers breathing life
'Brood-warm is the earth,
Lie close to its breast
Tranquil, the dewy pool
Hope gleams in soft waters
Vibrant this moorland air
Live and be glad'
Spring day on the high moor
The Day-Spring in my heart
And no more winter.

Ruth L Hartley

AN ISLAND CALLED TENERIFE

Let's go away somewhere
that is really exotic,
to a beautiful island,
some may call it Gothic.
We would fly on a plane
and land in Reina Sofia.
When you get there,
It will be your heart's desire.

> *We could go together*
> *and we'll never return,*
> *Not ever or ever or ever again.*

It will be somewhere hot and very sub-tropical.
The Quanches once lived here
on this wonderful island
where the tradition and folklore are very typical.
It's an island of beauty
called Tenerife.
And we could go to Puerto
or Los Cristianos,
Maybe the Valley of Oratava
or La Romantica with its magnificent aura.

> *We could go together*
> *and we'll never return,*
> *Not ever or ever or ever again.*

They call it the Land of Eternal Spring.
Everywhere you go there's an air of nostalgia.
It's a paradise on earth called Tenerife
And I know when you get there
you won't regret it.

This is the place that I call exotic.
Your heart's desire will be not to return here,
not ever or ever or ever again.

Rosalind Millar

A MOTHER'S LOVE

A mother's love, is a gift to be always treasured.
A mother's love, is never selfish, or unkind.
From a baby, cradled lovingly in protective arms
To an adult, a mother's love, stands the test of time.
Whenever you are in need, a mother's love is there.
Through sickness and unhappiness, this love is there to care.
A mother's love, never changes through the seasons.
A mother's love, stays constant through the years.
You may change, and sometimes other people too
But a mother's love, will always be around for you.
A mother's love, is there to give you comfort.
A mother's love, can lift you when you fall.
A mother's love, can take away the heartache.
A love, that doesn't choose which way to call.
It is easy, to take this love for granted.
It is easy, to awake and find it there.
Whatever love you share with a dear mother
Be grateful, that this love is there to share.
Precious, is the love that any mother gives.
Precious, to the young, and to the old.
A mother's love, can melt away the coldest heart.
A mother's love, won't leave you all alone.
A mother's love, will always be a part of you
Even if your mother is no longer there.
Your mother's love, will always be by your side.
This love, will be your precious guardian angel.
A love, that will never ever die.
A mother's love, will always be inside your heart
Forever beating until the end of time.

Michelle E Pickess

SEVENTEEN SUMMERS

I was just a young girl
When you fell into the empty space
Inside of me.
Stepping through my twenties
You picked the flowers as they grew.

If in the past you'd shown me affection
If you'd taken my heart with your record collection
It would be worse than it is.

C Stedman

MILLENNIUM POME

Where is the future of Logan's Run
The teleport and the laser gun
Soma. Protein pills. Black holes
The time machine of H G Wells?

Bionic men. Androids. Cyborgs
Interplanetary travel. Star Wars
Where are the ships that travel at the speed of light
Across the inky night?

Where are the warp drives
The Mega-Cities
Dan Dare
And Metropolis?
Where are all the Terminators
Flash
And Ming the Merciless?
Intelligent life from other worlds
Where are all the green-skinned girls
The Cybermen
The Mysterons
Where is Cpt Kirk and Major Tom?
Mr Clarke's Space Odyssey
The life that now I'm here was meant to be?

I feel cheated, duped and taken for a ride
That the science-fiction of my youth
Remains so in my life!

P Gray

GREENOCK

There's a town on the west coast of Scotland
A place I'd like to be,
To meet with friends and family,
And pals of yesteryear.
To visit all those places,
I played when I was young,
My heart fills up, I feel so proud,
I dream of the day I return.

To walk round the Cut in the summer,
Then carry on up to Loch Thom,
To sit in that beautiful setting,
It's all just a wonder to me.
I'm picturing all these places,
They're all in my memory,
It's the only place, I want to be,
It's home, sweet home, to me.

To Greenock, Greenock,
Named after the Green Oak Tree,
The town where I was born,
It's where I long to be.
It's Greenock, Greenock,
On the banks of the River Clyde,
I'll try so hard to get back there,
With my sweetheart by my side.

John Lindsay

THE BASIC QUESTION

On my progress as a pilgrim, I came to a first cross-roads
where men and women, clad in laboratory coats
worked over test tubes with the concentration
of teenagers at computer games, and I enquired:
          'Have you discovered the meaning of life?'
Then, one with a contemptuous snarl, answered:
          'We have no time to waste; we are scientists.
Move along and leave us to analyse our calculations.'

I came to a second cross-roads where stockmarket players,
stripped to open-necked shirts or blouses, moused
at internets, as intensely as bookmakers just as racehorses
set off, and I asked my question. 'We couldn't care less.
We are only concerned with profits for our shareholders.'

Then, on my pilgrimage, I reached a third cross-roads
where dons in academic robes sought to ensnare
further erudition with the single-mindedness
of a mole catcher on a damaged lawn. I queried.
          'Such is not within our remit. We are specialists.'

At length, my pilgrim tread reached a fourth cross-roads
where individuals brooded, apart, yet bonded
by soulful eyes, as if hearing through the silence
newly-created symphonic music; or lost in prayer.
I had to reiterate my question before one answered;
          'Stay with us for such is our concern
and your soul will flight from time into eternity
from Earth into infinite space, and you will blend
into our mutual, spiritual love and receive an answer,
wordlessly, expressing the meaning of life.'

Andrew Kerr

OLD MINERS

Yes, I was a miner and proud to do the work
Every day we left the earth to vanish underground,
To the dark and dusty world of Old King Cole
There we shovelled to keep this country warm
Now our lungs are full of dust
And no one wants to know
Of those proud old miners who kept this country great.
I walk around the valley, and see the miners there.
Faces grey and drawn, through lack of air
They sit and think of days gone by and how many
Butties will die before they get their just reward in
Heaven, I suppose.

Paul Derrick

STAND TALL . . .

Is there such a thing as an easy life
Where everything goes along smooth?
When you don't always have to struggle,
Or your worthiness constantly prove?
Where you don't need answers for everything?
When something's wrong, you're not always to blame?
Though possibly shallow self-confidence is why,
In those times they'll call your name.

But now is the time for you to stand tall
Be assertive and reach for the sky.
Search out what you want to achieve in your life
Stop letting things pass you by.
You've as much right as anyone to fulfil your dreams
Make up for all the lost time
Where you took all the slack, you took all the blame
Just being you seemed the crime.

Well, that time's passed, you're worth more than that,
You're no longer going to lie down,
Under people's snide comments and sarcastic remarks
For now in yourself you can find . . .
A tower of strength that breaks you free
From the chains that once held you still.
No longer shattered dreams in your heart
But wishes truly fulfilled.

Louise Sempey

EVEN THINGS KEPT IN JARS RUN OUT

My arm feels the space
next to me, days full
the night brings
countless remembered
exchanges.
Your T-shirt grows thin
with sniffing;
And memory-locked
distraction counts the
time in spite of
reason.

Alison Faulds

THE DINING ROOM

An abandoned chasm with ambitions of improvement
Changing room walls from a fleeting fad
Now shun their daring scheme
And crave a soothing cream to cool their eczema-ridden faces

Groaning, paint-speckled boards
Disturbed from years of covered peace
Now play clunky chimes to shod feet and canine claws
Pattering through the ever recurring particles
Of previous owner's workmanship

Where gossamer blue swathes once flamboyantly swirled
Around corkscrew arms
Now the windows are dressed by a scampering of busy weavers
In gossamer grey
And patterns not of my choosing.

The light bulb hangs
A tiny wolf-moon against a tawny false sky.

Diny van Kleeff

LATE EVENING

On a background canvas of azure blue
With shadowy clouds of greyest hue
Dappled shades of green, the sea
Lapping gently around the quay
Red sails captured in the evening sun
Deserted beach, day's activities done
Pebbles washed by the incoming tide
Seabirds swooping from every side
Playful shadows, sunset's kiss
An air of tranquillity and bliss
When all is still across the bay
This, is a magical time of day.

Iris Owen

INFERNAL ETERNALS

Driven through the hypothetical corridors of time
Avoiding the power traps in an order supposed,
A regimented hypocrisy of pathetic political lies
Never seen visionaries and corrupted royalties,
Defunct illusions and delusions of unchanging times,
Never believing the possibilities
Of a true necessity's need, the essentials ease
Souring our chance and notes of release,
Where is a justification's justice?
When dark pushers of greed destroy what we need
In the idea of what can be, as life comes and goes
We all can set free from our lives' circles
As moments' repercussions can last a lifetime
The boarders come down, diluted in one shared desire,
With each man beneath his ordinary load

All in the idea, in space and time
Freeing or chaining us all in a
Complete Subjective, Objective
Defeating the plagiarism of a false force's path

It's our beautiful calmness when the billions are as one
In cosmos' chaos because after all it's only cause and effect
Freedom comes in through the possibles,
In a singularity's continuous contradictions,
Crossing the dividing lines, amid a million signs

Our time's course is in our thoughts
On history's recyclable, yet
Navigable path, if we can find reasons why.
Seeing we're allowed to change.

Andrew Hawkins

FARMER'S PLIGHT

Cry. O' Land close to my heart,
The farmer has lost,
Cry, but not too much,
You do not know the cost,
You are out of touch,
The farmer must recreate or depart!

The little men in dark suits came,
Portenders of news better forgotten.
'You've got BSE, something is rotten!'
Declared the messengers of shame.

Reading reports, page after page,
The farmer went on a rampage,
Killing his precious cattle,
Holding tight in his saddle.

Tears in his eyes,
Anger in his heart,
Wife and children by his side,
Doom and despair in their cart.

The fires burnt and burnt,
Reflecting the farmer's hurt,
'Oh land of my fathers
My life lies in tatters!'

Clenched in his fists, another regulation, another demand,
Swinging from a branch, his neck in a harness
The farmer pays a last tribute to you, O' Land
His life ebbs away, his eyes staring into the darkness
Implore compassion from the little men,
Pity from God, forgiveness from his spouse and children.

How can a farmer cope? Is there any Hope?

Maria Thomas

THE HOME?

Staring blankly
Muttering
To people unseen
They sit
Around the walls
Mothers, Fathers,
Teachers, bosses
They were
Now nobody
Alone
Totally
Staring blankly
Muttering
Sitting endlessly

In the home?

Rachel M Aldrich

TIME

What's the time? I should be leaving
What's the time? Some more creeping
It's half-past ten my love,
No regrets my love.
What's the time? I should be leaving.

Just look outside and gaze around
Say goodbye, no, not a sound.
If they find out my love
Just give a shout my love.
Look outside and gaze around.

When I'm alone, I'll think of you,
When I'm down, don't know what to do.
O! Keep still my love,
Say you will my love.
When I'm alone, I'll think of you.

When I return, I'll make it plain,
When I return, be sure it's no game.
We'll be as one my love,
On our own, my love
When I return, I'll show it's no game.

B A Jones

THREE WISHES

Three wishes, three wishes,
You've only three wishes.
Think carefully what you will choose.
Marie wants a rabbit,
A dog and a hamster,
Elaina, long nails, chips and gold.
Nathaniel chose robots,
A football and TV
To watch in his room on his own.
Pete thinks he'll send e-mails,
Go internet surfing;
His sister's despatched to the moon.
Everyone else longs for
Millionaires' palaces.
Designer clothes, fast cars and yachts.
That just leaves Anita
Who's patiently waited
To share her three wishes, as well.
Mid nudges and whispers
And looks of derision
She bravely ignores their disdain.
In her washed see-through dress
With its drooping, frayed hem.
She pours out her longing and pain.
I've only two wishes,
The third one's not needed.
If I can have two, that's enough.
I wish that my house was
Like other people's, and
I wish my dad could be in it.

Jean Howard

AIRS AND GRACES

I'll give you a
Piece of my mind
If you will promise
Me a lasting
Peace of mind.
I'll give up my
Airs and graces
If you will promise
That I shall be
Heir to graces
Hitherto unknown.
I may be no
Better than I should be
But you should
Make a better me.
The hole in my heart
To change - a
Whole-hearted lover
Of life to rise
And shine -
A new essential me.

Wendy Kellett

MANY HAPPY RETURNS

'Why do you cry little girl?' the old man said,
'I cry for you,' she raised her head,
'Your back is bent, you look so cold,
It's not very nice, when you grow old
All your bones ache, so I've been told!
You hair has almost disappeared,
Your teeth have gone,
But you've grown a beard.
You walk so slowly across the floor,
But I never heard you open that door,
Please Sir tell me how you did that trick?
You look quite pale, are you sick?'
The old man sat, as if to rest awhile,
The puzzled young girl gave him, the sweetest smile,
'I think you look like someone I love;
But the Lord took him up above,
Please Sir tell me, please explain
How you look almost, the very same.'
'I'm your grandad who passed away,
Back to ask you, for my soul, to pray,
A message for your mum and dad,
Tell them I'm happy, don't be sad,
Wipe that tear from your eye,
I don't ever want to see you cry,

Peter James Hawley

TORTURED SLEEP

My death has come to me at last
In slumber dreaming of the past
I awoke just once and beheld a demon
The hideous features brought my scream on.
Back years and years this timeless dream
Yet all is not as it would seem
Past, present and future fuse together
The crashing sea, the stormy weather
And in my slumber I realise
The twisted face, the tortured eyes
The demon I did recognise
'Tis me, a dead and lifeless one
From this earth now I have gone
Through lifeless eyes and in a daze
I see my father's unearthly gaze
Ten years past he went afore me
Now I see him stand before me
Unaltered by time
And yet his hand I must decline
I scream, 'No I'm not ready'
Even though I feel unsteady
I flee from this haunted tomb
And find myself back in my room
'Just a bad dream - of that I'm certain
The demon emerges from behind the curtain.'

Paul John Hutchinson

WHY?

What do you think of in that place beyond the sky?
Do you remember us at all as we ask the reason why?
You took away our light, our laughter and our fun
And went to join those folks on high, you self-deluded one.

Were you standing there among us, us poor grieving mortal souls?
Did you feel the pained reaction to the music that was played?
As we stood in shock remembering; puzzled and dismayed.
You made us sad and angry, and frustrated and alone.
You dared to take your perfect life
But with it took our own.
Did you think the world a better place, if you took your leave and left?
Well, listen to the cries of the mourning and bereft.

You were the party animal, the leader of the pack.
The adored by many, the pal, the son
The charismatic one.
I expect the pain will lessen and your name will be forgot
Within the next millennium, but then again, p'raps not.

I hope you are at peace now
And I hate you if you are.
How could you in your arrogance expect us not to care?
To carry on regardless without a thought or prayer?
Did you think so little of us
Or did you just not think at all?

If I make it up to Heaven in several decades' time,
Have the party ready, the music and the wine.
But do me one last favour from your mansion in the air,
Meet me in my dreams tonight and let me know you care.
Don't worry about us down below, we'll get along just fine
And you can give us answers in the great fullness of time.

Anne Graham

KELLING HEATH, NORFOLK

Blackbird and pigeon announcing the dawning,
I open my door to the bright golden morning.
Along sandy lanes with canine friend Bingo,
With joy in our footsteps we enter the meadow.

Butterflies flitter with never a care,
Meadow browns, common blues, jewelling the air.
We wade through the ragwort and ripe-seeded grass,
And grasshoppers spring from our feet as we pass.

Entering the quiet cathedral of woodland
Beneath the tall oak, fir and beech trees we stand.
Beech mast floor dappled with shifting bright patterns,
Dense fronds of bracken fern on either hand.

The pool with its lilies and tall rustling rushes,
Where roach, carp and stickleback lazily swim,
Is home to a myriad of bright blue damselflies
Whirring and darting o'er surface and rim.

Home through the vibrant and heat-hazed heather,
The gorse sings its praise to the hot August weather.
Was there ever a place that is nearer to Heaven
Than Kelling Heath Park? We will love you forever!

Doreen Lawrence

SUMMER HOLIDAY

Stretched on golden sand
My body tingles with the sun,
As once it tingled to your touch,
My lips are burning with remembered kisses,
Kisses that I want so much,
Oh now I long for your caress,
Time doesn't ease the memories,
Or distance making the longing less;
Seabirds wheel in sunlit skies,
But I can only see your eyes,
And feel again your fingers in my hair;
All around the sounds of summer
Floating on the fragrant air,
The cry of gulls, the splash of waves,
As seas caress the shore,
As gentle as the touch of hands
That woke my body to its first desire,
Warmer than the sun your lips,
They set my very soul on fire,
And kissed the innocence of youth away,
Within your arms that summer day.

Ailsa Keen

MRS FARLEY'S

I thumbed down the well-worn latch on the door
The door bottom scraped on the stone-flagged floor
A bell chimed somewhere deep within
Then a big step down, and we were in.

The room was small and dark inside
As usual our eyes were open wide
We took all in, that welcome smell
Of sweets and chocolate we loved so well

Mrs Farley wasn't there
We waited on the wooden chair
Rocked back and forth as we knew we could
Uneven flags knocked stone on wood

As if by magic she appeared
Happy to see us, calling us dears
My sister and I and our pennies each
In a Donegal town, on our way to the beach

Ann Beggs

MICKY JOES

Micky Joes picked his nose
He picked the dirt between his toes
He picked his cuts until they bled
And picked his ear at night in bed

Said Mrs Joes
'Blow your nose
Clean the dirt between your toes
Cover your cuts and they'd never have bled
And go to sleep at night in bed.'

So Micky Joes blew his nose
Cleaned the dirt between his toes
Covered his cuts that never bled
But didn't sleep at night in bed
He picked his belly button instead

Said Mrs Joes 'Don't pick your belly
As sure as goodness you'll turn to jelly
You'll melt down upon the floor
And there'll be no Micky anymore.'

But Micky picked and picked his belly
And right enough he turned to jelly
Melted down upon the floor
And Picky Micky was no more.

> *Moral of story*
> *Don't pick!*

Elaine Lavery

THE PLACE

Here all is structured
Scroll of stone and carved leaf
Follow the line of patterned stillness
And with raised and pitted bark of tree trunk
Stand forth uncluttered, in relief

Here all evasions
Fail before truth's strong-riven word
Writ slowly in accepting tissue
Incising without error, order
The Opus Dei for life's record

So, so incise each place we reach
That when relentless comes the night
We feel, O thou who brought us to this place
The grain of truth beneath the fingers
Unalterable, however change the light

Marion Payne

MY MIND

My mind's a raging torrent
With many depths unknown
So shallow on the surface
Yet I'm drowning in its hold
Elated puffed contentment
Ironic flat despair
Impaired by open vision
And judgement that's not there
Nor comfort from surrounding
Of fallen graces found
A tumour so forbidding
Of sight and touch and sound
Extinguishes my senses
And within my eyes I cry

Patricia Moss

SPACE TRAVELLER

Could I but don the wings of space and time
And fly to realms beyond our planet Earth,
Or ride perhaps, upon a comet's tail
To circumnavigate our daytime star
The Sun. And then take flight to Saturn's rings,
A jewel in the crown of solar spheres.
But I must travel on into the void
Where bold Orion's stars call silently
To view his treasure house of glowing gas
And youthful suns his stellar nursery hides.
From here my wings are spurred to further flight
To galaxies beyond our Milky Way,
Each with a thousand million stars that shine
As sparkling chandeliers on every hand,
And sun-like stars that beam their golden light
Upon each retinue of planet forms.
But will I find another earth-like sphere
With seas and woods and all familiar things,
And creatures like ourselves who think and dream,
And question on this wondrous universe?
Perhaps, perhaps, in ages yet to come
We may have sight of beings like ourselves.
But now I must return to planet Earth,
For I am human form, and this my home.

John Wilson Smith

WHERE HAVE ALL THE BIRDS GONE?

Where have all the birds gone?
I would really like to know.
I used to hear all manner of early-morning songs,
But it seems that those days have long-gone.
I hear plenty of rooks and raucous crows too,
But I would like to hear the skylark, nightingale, wouldn't you?
I've tried feeding and watering, leaving out nuts and seeds,
Aren't any of today's birds in any sort of need?
It's not just in my garden that I miss all these sights,
But also when I walk my dogs, morning, noon or night.
When I was a child, not so long ago,
You could hear any amount of birdsong all around you know,
It's not that I'm not listening, because I sit quietly for hours,
But it seems the birds have flown or at least they're not ours.
I haven't any cats to put them off a visit,
I also try to cater for all requisites,
But all to no avail.
I really do love my garden and to have feathered visitors,
Would make me very happy.
It's not as if a bird can read,
So I can't put up a sign 'Free seed'.
But I do hope that come the spring,
I'll get some feathered friends and a few of their offspring.
I've not lived here for very long, only half a year,
But at my other residence I had whole families of birds living near.
A blackbird came in daily for a digestive biscuit,
And didn't I get in trouble if I forgot and missed it!
She would come into the house and chirrup and flap her wings,
As if to say 'I'm more important, stop doing other things.'
When I left my old place, I issued out a plea,
To the new owners 'Please, look after my birds for me!'

People say I'm silly to be so concerned.
But if we all took the time and trouble to look after more than
just ourselves.
The world would be a nicer place,
For everything, including the human race.

E Carter

PRECIOUS SPECIES

I can see why you are inclined to think
That maybe you are the lucky one,
When you travel from the cluster
As I had once done.
Departing blindly oblivious, to anything or anyone,
Hurtling towards an uncertain fate.
I hurt you perhaps, when I refuse to make you feel welcome?

Love beads?
You wear me down.
But you eventually abandon your presumptuous thread.
You emerge once a month, in death,
Wretchedly accusing me of indifference.
As I too accuse you
Of wasting my time.

I cannot see a need for all this.
I will never hold you,
(As I never held the others).
You will never become.
And I refuse to wear your so-called perfection
Round the neck of my being like a precious jewel,
Shimmering in its reflected glory.

Rashida Khatun-Uddin

FACING THE FACTS

Having made love, we sleepily talk in whispers,
Thinking that no one will know what we have been doing.
But the look on our faces says it all.
We glow like the embers in a fire, and our self-satisfied faces shine like
sunlight on sparkling waters.
We think love,
We talk love,
We make love.
But this *must* always remain *our* secret.
No one knows but *you* and *I*
(and those who can read faces!)

Ashley K Howard

TINGES OF AUTUMN

Crisp fingers and toes bite the morning air
Sunlight shimmers on golden trees
Flame leaves saunter to their rustling carpet, a winter bed for
little creatures.
Lying low the washed sun awakens and exerts himself to show a
pallid face.
Berries ripen full and true, a forthcoming winter feast.
A flight of birds arrows across the clear blue yonder.

Stella Graham

SPECIAL LADY

My mother,
Focus of my childhood
An unconditional love
Proud to call her 'Mam',
My mother.

My mother
The home-maker
Endless support and encouragement
The hand that guided the way
My mother.

The tables now have turned,
The years march on
Taking their toll on
My lovely 'Mam',
My mother.

The mind plays cruel tricks
She no longer remembers
She slows her step, her thoughts are lost
But I'm still proud to call her 'Mam',
My mother.

Ann Nall

LIFE

Life is like the sea
It comes in small ripples to the shore
It is like life's trails creeping up on us
The pitfalls and errors we cannot see
They come like waves big and small
Big and small our troubles seem
Until we call on the Lord
We put our hand in His
And draw strength from the Lord
And if we pray and humble ourselves
And give Him our faith in Him
And put on our armour He will love us
Care love and heal us He is the Lord

C Carr

ANGELUS

Merciless sun pounding hard on my back
As I walk the track trodden by a thousand generations
Upward I climb with effort soaking my skin
My heart crashing, breath dragging in out
And then I stop
Breath lost completely
As I ingest the sheer beauty
Of what is handed to me
As I reach the top
The turquoise world undulates before my eyes
Turns dark and brooding
The further out it stretches
And it stretches forever

I sink to my knees and worship
Nature, wild, untameable -
Ceaseless eternal waves
That beat and bruise ragged rocks
With the power of thunder,
Remorselessly -
Gulls wheeling and screaming
Filling my senses
With flashes of white
As the foam rises toward me
Never-ending scene of perfection absolute
As emerald hues envelop and overwhelm me
I realise this is my church
And here will I worship forever

Jill Shepherd

SPARE ANY CHANGE MATE?

The invisible man. A dishevelled disgrace.
You won't look in my face.
Spare any change mate?

Won't give me your copper. I know what you think
- I'll spend it on drink
Spare any change mate?

But, do you go down the pub when you've had a bad day?
What more can I say?
Spare any change mate?

A successful young man. That could've been me
But you choose not to see.
Spare any change mate?

Battered senseless by Dad, Mum couldn't care less.
My life in a mess.
Spare any change mate?

An existence of fear. No loving, no giving.
I'm so tired of living.
Spare any change mate?

Driven out on the street. Still living in fear.
Not my choice to be here.
Spare any change mate?

The life of a beggar is so degrading.
My will is fading.
Spare any change mate?

Body wracked with disease and no strength left to fight -
think I'll call it a night.
Spare any change mate?

One more unmarked grave to add to the list.
I didn't exist.
No change needed?

J C Fishwick

AS I LIE HERE

As I lie here I think only of you
The fun and the love
But what did you do?
You grew bored, said you'd had enough
How can you have enough of someone's love?

Love is a drug
You just need to find the right dealer
One who has the mix right
To keep you happy day and night
You sold me a rough mix

When I questioned what you did
You said that's your lot - that's it
You left me to go cold turkey
You took everything I loved
But I'm still here

Through the crap you threw at me
I learned to survive
To hold my head up high
And now I'm dealing with the main man
And thank God it's him.

My life is addictive
I can't live without that
I can't live without this

I must have that
I must do this
I have to love
I have to hold
I have to cry
I have to breathe
I have to die
I have to be born again
I have to show you

There's alternatives my friend
And my beautiful life will one day end
In the most addictive place ever
It's called heaven

Paul Carter

K S L I JUNGLE WARFARE TRAINING 1967
(A challenge to the artist)

Like corrugated iron they ripple on.
The resonant Australian voices claim
That lost or sick, half-starving or bewildered,
We only need to look about to see
That the jungle's an immense dispensary,
A map of the map, 'a bloody great green salad'.
So long as we can stand we can survive.

No one doubts we can and will survive;
Survive the swamp which swallows up our sweat,
Outlive our thin chameleon uniforms
Torn on the insistent 'waitawhile',
Break the belukar,
Curse and hack, break out of the belukar,
Survive that first ambush,
Thought of, dreamed of, seen in detail, sprung;
Recreated long before it happens.
It is so easy.
All this is just a choice 'twixt life and death,
A trial of strength, an appeal to reflexes.

But in the last light of a jungle base-camp
The quiet and peacefulness are relative.
Slender plants and saplings shake and quiver
As raindrops splash from the living canopy.
The fallen leaves begin to phosphoresce,
Diminutive portents of an after-life.
Cold consciences are dimly preyed upon
By an ill-defined translucent form of fear
Like palely frosted glass before the moon
Standing between ourselves and certainty.

I think the artist might depict this wraith,
Stalking between these men and the tall trees,
As something cerebral in casual spaces,
A shadow with depth, a face among the faces.

Jeremy York

SKY

I lift my head up to the sky,
to watch the clouds
as they sail by,
The different blues
a shared delight,
As the darkest blue seem to fade to white
I pause awhile
I blink my eyes
the blues no more just pretty pink sky
The sun goes down,
in creeps the dark,
the sky's so quiet but for the lark.

Irene Draper

THE HIRAETH OF ETERNITY
(In Memory of R S Thomas)

Not that you doubted the holes in His side -
But where was the caring, loving God?
Silent, invisible and as awesome
As some black hole on the edge of a
Far-flung galaxy? Or so it must have seemed

Until now, when the *hiraeth* of eternity
Called to you across the infinite spaces
And bore you to a new, uncharted land
Where - with the rocks, birds and the seas -
You may be taught to sing a gentler song.

Richard Leigh Harris

LIQUID GOLD
(Dedicated to my cousin - lost on Piper Alpha)

Sitting here thinking about all the oil exploration.
What will become of all its cruel and vast devastation?

When all the drills stop turning and breaking-up our
ocean plates - who will be responsible for all its terrible
and real fates.

These floating, towering structures of power await in our
seas, in our lives to devour - men's lives toll to pay the price
in return for all their trouble and strife!

Where will it end, God only knows and then they sink
another hose, to suck up yet another sample of this
crude thick - black, liquid-vamping!

This criminal process - sucking the blood of the sleeping
ocean, what will Mother Nature replace with this potion?

Day by day the seabed gets drier, who realises or cares to
hear her crying? In vain she cries, *stop* - you are upsetting
your domain and you in the end will feel the strain! When
no longer my ocean plates can take it, the earth will shake,
don't say I mistake it!

The coming of earthquakes, you can be assured, more lives
will toll for this liquid - now obscure! The towering, powerful
structures will drown and who cares - what - in for a penny - a pound!

Money will no longer be of concern and one will start to think of
the harm - these advanced techniques and equipment have brought -
and something to replace it will be sought!

The coming of oil has its pros and cons - what will you think - when
it is over - *gone!*

Jan Bremner

UNLOVED?

We have all tasted the bitterness of life
Marooned in a space bereft of love,
Hungry for the world to know of our existence,
Souls in torment reaching out for a reason for our being.
Do we not exist, are we a figment of own imaginations,
Do we not really feel, do we not bleed, do we not laugh,
Do we not cry. Is this because we are unloved, this feeling
as cold as a mountain stream,
We are as a dark silent world awaiting the rising of the sun.
A soul incomplete because we are unloved, or are we the victims
of negative thought.

Eileen Jones

I: WRITES I

To save myself . . . I write -
But never diaries: that kind would get too close
To seeing my real self. It's for others alone I write
And type, etch, scribble, scratch, make signs. At observations
I'm good, can capture exact a refracted shadowed obstructed light
Poems allow me dowries of self-indulgence -
Freed verse, syllabics polyrhythmic accents that seduce
And converge to unstiffen still lives like my silent palette . . .
While I'm fairly fine at perspective, I feel bare thoughts
Are where I'm best, And since, at times, I wish
Others would share their innernesses,
Have to stay content with newspapers and photographs
For company. With cleared precisions
My strokes pen in the spacings with forms of light
That cover my papers and wastes of naked white;
I write as if possessed between narrowed lines
That loneliness and duty have placed before my eyes
To draw in yet another's gaze that frames
My sight, itself a stilled slave in a landscape of vanities;
I write to make appearances seem and sound sane
Filling out the faked wounds that ooze pain
The pain, the panic, the pretence; with precision
I write to make up for her lack of attention . . .

Jules Lovenbury

MAKEOVER

Can I have a makeover and
a new personality.
Can I just be clean and sober
and a mind with high capacity.
I want to sound articulate and promising.
Girls then will see I'm immaculate and
the handsomest thing.
Can I have a new brain and beauty to go with.
Then I know I'll never be the same and someone
will suit me, and love I can give.

A makeover is exactly what I need.
So come on adolescence proceed.
When I reach twenty-one.
I can show people that I'm a lot of fun.
But now just being fourteen.
I remain like in prison.
I know somewhere in-between people
will sit up and listen!

Simon Hart

CLAN CAMPBELL'S GOLD

In the dawning, my love is winging, with her white sail
o'er the ocean now she's coursing. Shining armour and
spear points gleaming; the battle's over, now of red wine
we are dreaming.

Whilst on her timbers, lie new scars of battle and in her hold
now lie Clan Campbell's cattle. So sing MacDonald, rejoice
Clan Ranald with your comrades true and bold for in your hands
you have Clan Campbell's gold.

No dreams of war now, her wings are folded and Clan Campbell's
chieftain, like a child newly scolded. Then in the evening, the swan
is flying beside, my true love now my heart is softly sighing. And in
the morning once more she's coursing and in my heart's blood then
the joy is freely flowing.

Shining armour and spear points gleaming; the battle's looming
soon of red wine we'll be dreaming.

Ron Greer

TWO OUT OF THREE IS BAD

I hate triangles because
Two into three leaves
One left out:
Because three-sided objects
Point to an unresolved
Piggy-in-the-middle:
I hate triangles because
They're theoretically symmetrical
But never are,
And because the sum of two sides
Is never equal to the agony
Of the third.

Kate Appleby

THE MIRROR

When I was little I looked into
A mirror, and realised there
Were two of me.
One here, and one there;
One there, and one here.
Everything I would do, she
Would do too. And everything
She would do, I would try
To copy. I would smile,
And she would smile back.
She would laugh, and I would
Laugh along too.
I noticed she had a room just
Like mine, she even had the
Same toys.
One day I decided I
Would swap places with
Her, and that night I
Dreamt that I stepped into
The mirror, and into her
Identical room. She did the
Same, and we waved to
Each other when we were
Both safely across.
In the morning when I awoke
I rushed to the mirror where
The other me was already waiting.

We looked about us, and we
Agreed that everything still looked
The same. But as I looked
Down at my toes, I realised
That my slippers were on the
Wrong feet, and I knew
That it hadn't been a dream.

Maria Phillips

STEADFASTNESS

In serving the Lord,
One sets one's own standard
From which one will not shrink
And go over the brink
But will be steadfast
and hold onto one's mast.

It is the flag of sincerity
Which will blow in all eternity
And stand up to any wind.
Not even the hurricane with its spin
Will uproot its mast
For its purpose is steadfast.

M MacDonald-Murray

HOPE

I am numb, incoherent
My form controlling me
A mass of confusion
See this mask of forced perfection
Raw betrayal hidden behind this facade
People all around
Why don't they hear
Screaming
Mouth open wide
Despair is so consuming
Not a single glance
No one hears
Intensely searching
Hope within my grasp
drinking gulping it down hard and fast
almost fearful to swallow
sensuous hope.

Emma Scott-Smith

A LANCASTER BOMBER'S FLIGHT ENGINEER
IN PRAISE OF MERLIN ENGINES

Roar on you mighty 'Merlins'
Run *sweet* and falter not.
For every missing heartbeat
Ties my stomach in a knot.

Roar on you mighty Merlins
Six lives depend on you.
On smoothly gliding piston
And air-devouring *screw*.

Roar on you mighty Merlins
Lift us straining off the *deck*.
Past dimly lit control tower
And blazing *'Lankie'* wreck.

Roar on you mighty Merlins
Through the night sky inky-black
Homing on our target
Jinking through the flak.

Roar on you mighty Merlins
Bombs away comes clear and loud
Then we're climbing and we're *banking*
And we're racing for the cloud.

Roar on you mighty Merlins
Take us high and straight and fast
Outrun those waiting vultures
With their deadly cannon blast.

Roar on you mighty Merlins
Through the day-break's eerie light
Cross steely channel waters
And the Dover cliffs so white.

Roar on you mighty Merlins
Over Kentish fields and streams
And babies stirring in their cots
Awakened from their dreams.

Roar on you mighty Merlins
Now our *field* lies straight ahead
Criss-crossed by blazing Verey lights
Of white and green and red.

Roar on you mighty Merlins
As we touch-down on our drome
Then rest you trusty engines
For you've brought us safely home.

Derek Williams

SEQUENCE ON SATURDAY

Often through loneliness many come here
seeking new company to dance away the years.
Face to face they waltz or sway to the tango,
elegant in stance, hypnotised by rhythm.
Silly lights flicker with imitation stars;
coloured skirts flare in swirls of abandon;
beats of the Cha Cha, sultry rumba girations;
dancing in sequence, gregarious delight;
stylish new hair perms, white crowns in the light;
line-dancing to old tunes, regimental processions
'Waltz over Texas', 'The Cowboy Charleston'!
They sing together, social barriers forgotten,
then return from the shadows to realities again.
Confidences may be shared with easy acquaintance;
artificial laughter may be loud to convince,
but all are determined in pursuit of some joy,
reluctant to return to emptiness.
The last waltz, sentimental recall,
loneliness emphasised by maudling memory.

R Midwinter

WINTER'S APPROACH

September nights darken early now,
And ripened fruit is falling,
Friends gather at the harvest show,
Warm summer days recalling.

October's golden glow is fading,
Leaves change from green to darker hue,
The farmer tends the final baling,
Skies turn to grey where once were blue.

November and the bonfire blazes,
Children rosy in the firelight glare,
Steamy breath on window glazes,
With morning fog on frosty air.

December now and much more jolly,
Windows gay and coloured lights ablaze,
Anticipation of the festive frolic,
The Christ-child's birthday soon to celebrate.

Peggy Norton

ALL IS WELL

And so it comes to an end
Only stories I say
Don't worry,
I love you,
You've always got me
Always,
My sweetest
Goodnight!

Christopher Casswell (11)

I REFUSE

I refuse to grow old
Because I am the future
And when did the future grow old?

Conclusions

Conclusions are illusions
And this is a conclusion.

Litska Rodèf

WHO AM I?

There are many sides of me, I think,
Some know me as one and some another.
At times I am strong and can help the weak.
At times I am weak and need the strong -
Who am I?
There are days, even weeks when I close myself in,
When no one can enter my innermost thoughts -
These times can be depressing.
Days when I open out and share with all
What I feel, the joy, the wonders of living -
Who am I?
I cannot change completely, I am what I am,
Although many times I do try to be the
Happy person with kind thoughts of all,
But alas, this does not last.
There is no one perfect, how could there be,
Even if there were, this place no happier could be.
We are all, what we are, an individual person, complete,
But I still wonder . . .
        Who am I?

Heather G Wilkinson

A CATCH OF A BAT?

One hot summer's day,
Under the children's bed,
My man he found a bat
He tried to catch it,
After several attempts
He caught it,
He ran down the stairs,
Like a stork carrying a baby
At arm's length he held it
We all ran after him down the street
To see the catch of a bat.

Finally arriving at the green,
Over the wall he gently shook it,
To set it free,
We all had to have a look,
It lay there, lifeless.
A closer look revealed it all,
'It's a black rotten banana!'
Shouted my brother,
We all screamed with laughter.

A Bhambra

ONLY A MOTHER KNOWS

Look into her eyes;
slate-grey pools of dew - wandering - glistening under artificial light.
Her mouth twitches - smooth, round cheeks rise to her smile -
out time, the solitude of night.

Listen to her coo;
animated features fill her tiny face - rag doll body wrapped around my
naked skin.
Every facial muscle used, to express those unknown feelings she holds
deep within.

Is she real?
Empty! Lonely! Vulnerable! Emotions devour my body with such
power;
a tidal wave of nausea - eyes fill like tulips, drenched in a
springtime shower.

'Let down' - hold me;
seconds pass, feelings subside - breasts tingle - tight - tender to touch,
aching to be drained - dripping softly onto her cheek -
nipple within her clutch.

Look at her mouth;
tongue searching between open lips - cupid's bow laced with dimples,
threaded with rubies.
Rooting, snuffling - muffled sounds of satisfaction - locates, latches -
contented sneeze.

Gaze into her eyes;
translucent spheres of crystal - visualise her future - imagine how
she grows.
Pure perfection, caressed by another - panic, fear, grief - only a
mother knows.

Susan Seward

LOW TAR, HIGH TAR, AVATAR - HOLY SMOKE

'It's cool' they say 'To smoke' they say,
Those young and budding girls,
who puff their fags just like old lags,
and burn their lives away.
'It may be cool to smoke' I say
'In your young and simple minds,
But it's also hot, as hot as hell,
When you burn behind the blinds,
In all those coffins made of wood,
of wood of many kinds.
Why follow in the steps of stupid men,
Who smoked as many as they may,
Who copied Grant and Bogart,
Who smoked at work and play.
There are no role models *like* them,
About the world today.
So why do you smoke those tubes of death,
Whose danger is proclaimed
On the packet that contains them,
And through the media famed!
Surely not to kill yourselves at such an early age,
And make your lovely rose-red lips
Smell like a stinking chimney,
Or a filthy monkey's cage!
So give them up you silly girls,
And think about your future -
Not cancerous growths within yourselves,
And suture after suture!'

Anthony Chamberlaine-Brothers

THE VENDOR

The biting wind,
the howling screech of it,
whirling the old newspapers around the stand.
He sits there
day after day.
His punters know,
rain, hail or snow,
he sits there,
the cold, hard seat his second home.
His face is blank
until the obligatory smile
cracks the weather-beaten lines.
His mind ever active,
no rest.
The headlines are his breakfast, lunch
- a daily feast that sets the cogs in motion.
A tireless journey through the problems of the world,
an endless search for all the answers.
A mind in turmoil,
arguing each point from every angle.
- Telegraph!
- 40p, Son.

Karen Barron

YOUNG AT HEART

I may be old
but I don't care
as long as I
can climb the stairs.

I do keep fit
I ramble too
and that's what
fit folk ought to do.

It keeps your mind
off other things
a lot of pleasure
too it brings.

Across those fields
one walks with zest
properly attired
and map on chest.

One walks for miles
and oh what joy
you meet a friend
a real nice boy.

The moral of
this little tale
is up and go
if not too frail.

Eline Ottewell

BEING BLIND

When I was blind I could not see anything around me
No trees, no flowers, nor the sky, nor the sea
I had to use my other senses to help me see.
Like my ears to hear, my hands to feel
My nose to smell and my tongue to taste.
My senses help me but you my friend
Can be my eyes to describe the things all around me.

Alexander W Kelly (5)

BLACK ROSE

Black rose,
Lost your blood,
Cloaked in thorns,
Hide from the hand that plucks,
Grow gracefully within your place,
Symbolise a life of pity and pain,
Let the rain wash it away,
Quench your thirst,
And grow again.

Eleanor Rose Markham

THE GIVER

I feel replenished in
The wake of Her beam
Of hope and goodness
I am lucky to see
This rainbow of light that
Appears at dawn before dark
Without Her I would lose
My wake up spark
Birds awaken through Her
Marvellous call
Her soft caressing touch
Blesses our home
Which
Revolves around light
And the life She brings
Her generous gift takes care
Of my being
Just think, one spot in our sky
Is one of thousands
We are passing by
How though small,
Important She is!
This little, big treasure
Is for us to live!

Caroline Peate

CRAWLEY DOWN FOOTBALL CLUB

In that summer they dropped the 'Village', to our regret,
And headed for the summit
Thwarted only by the lack of lights:
And so, themselves thwarted,
And full of ambition and successful moves,
Moved on the heart of keeper, midfield and attack
The first I knew was another team's newspaper report
Of course, things were not the same
I would still walk up the hill on Saturdays
(Early kick-offs in the winter - no lights)
Especially when the Reds flirted briefly with relegation:
I had no desire to follow the turncoats
Although I'd be lying if I said they were the only team I've ever liked
It's more modest now
And even if a time comes
Of more success
It won't be the same
You don't lose your heart
And not notice.

Lawrence Long

FARMYARD REVOLT

The Rooster and Flock were strutting around,
Eating their corn in their own little pound,
When along came the Rabbit, Weasel and Stoat,
Watching with envy; they were joined by the Goat,
'Can we partake?' they chorused as one,
'Because where we live it isn't much fun.'
'But of course,' said the Rooster, strutting with pride,
'Our house is your home, we've nothing to hide.'
'Hold on, hold on,' said the Hen with a scowl,
'Who next will come in, the Eagle the Owl?
We've barely enough to last us the year,
If we share what we got, it will cost us so dear.'
'Nonsense,' said the Rooster, with a shake of his head,
'You cackle too much, I'll forget what you said.'

As time passed by the Rabbits increased,
The jolly old Rooster, well now, he's deceased,
The Goat ate the grass as much as he could,
The Weasel stole plenty, as the Hen knew he would,
The Stoat prowled the pound eating the eggs,
And chasing the flock till they were run off their legs.

'At last,' said the Hens, 'enough is enough,
Since this lot arrived we've had it so rough,
Our homes have been taken and food we have none,
Our Rooster is dead and left us with no son.'
So huddled together with a whisper and moan,
They decided as one, to recapture their home,
'Leave' said the Hen, to the overfed Goat,
'And take with you also the Weasel and Stoat.'
'No' smirked the Rabbit with utter disdain,
'It's you who must leave, you're becoming a pain.
From when we arrived up till now,
You've done nothing but moan just like a cow,
We are now many and you are so few,
And we've become strong, there's nowt you can do.'
'Wrong' said the Hen, 'we too have grown,

And now it's time to take back our home.'
As if on cue the flock did appear,
From all ports they came front, side and rear,
'Charge' squawked the Hen, 'the time is at hand,
To take back our homes and regain our land.'

When the feathers had settled and fighting was done,
The flock looked around and knew they had won,
'So Chicken all over to you, this I do say,
Before you have guests make sure they pay.'

David Anthony Howard

UNEXPECTED ENCOUNTER

Arrive behind a garage, which is opposite an off-licence
A man in black coat, with professional concern
Says 'I'm sorry the bruise on the left side is showing
Will you kindly come in.'
'Please' I think 'will someone explain?'

The door swings open and I step inside
The air is scented, smells of death.
Leaning forward through the haze that surrounds me
The room lacks light
And I have a feeling of dread.

There it is, confronting, in front of me,
Resting idyllically on wrought iron stands
Brass plate on the top and also brass handles
The contents I think, 'I know what they are!'
And the feeling of dread turns ever deeper.

Standing alone, wishing for company
I quietly approach, then look inside.
My mind screams out 'Christ! He really *is* dead!'
And a part of me notes, in detached observation,
'He's right, the bruise on the left side does show.'

Wanting to run from the face with the confusion
To hide from the fact that he really is dead
Believing the papers and television lied
To wake one morning and laugh at the sick joke.
But I know I must stay, for I'll hear that laughter never.

I know now my dreams will be haunted and my conscience awakened
And all that I do, I'll think 'Did he do it too?'
To suddenly be an only child, now a family of three
I shudder, lean over, take one last look
And then, wish him 'Goodbye.'

Ray Simpson

SPRING

Spring is upon us once again
Winter has not been all in vain
For underneath her coat of snow
She's hiding colours all aglow.

Isn't spring a lovely sight?
Filling the earth with such delight
Daffodils blooming, primroses too
As we stir out of our beds,
The snowdrop nodding her sleepy head.

Spring is mellow, spring is sweet
Sets our feet dancing and animals a-prancing
Oh what joy spring is here
Thank God for *spring*.

F D Fellows

FORGOTTEN ANGELS

Forgotten angels who play at love's game
Who crave for heroes in pleasure or shame
Making their fortunes and masking their fame
Only living for now and dying without flowers.

Forgotten angels in some shady bar
She may dance for your pennies whoever you are,
You may hold her near but she'll never go farther
Than a room with a bed with the wallpaper faded
Only living for now and dying without flowers.

Somebody's sister, maybe somebody's Ma
Who aimed at the bright lights of some distant star
Who was never at home in a love-nest for two
But cried for attention, long overdue.

Forgotten angels who have never known love
Who have warm, golden bodies most men dream of
Who can never be held in one man's embrace
Who sell you their bodies with no smile on their faces
Only living for now and dying without flowers.

Albert Edward Reed

DON'T LOOK

Try not to look for troubles in this world,
If you do, you will surely find it,
Don't even think you have the flu or mumps
The chance is that you will have it
So smile along this path in time and enjoy the present,
Go on! Make the best of each new day
And life you will find can be pleasant.

Janet Dennis

RECIPE FOR AUTUMN

Neatly ploughed fields,
dishes of
brown porridge - well stirred.
Dusted with white gulls.

Yellowing, elderly hedgerows,
jewelled with
rich purple, red and orange.
Robbed by greedy crows.

Misty, damp mornings,
hints of
orange, becoming purple afternoons,
Dark-cloaked by early evenings.

Karlen Lawrence

MOBILEPHONEAPHOBIA

Panics on at Panasonic
Quick pace no place for mistakes
This work place takes breaks
To rejuvenate juvenile delinquents, foreign immigrants,
Year out students, arduous aunts
All taught to dance in time
With the assembly line
And ten minutes every two hours
Is how a first class work force
Is rewarded before it gets back
To stacking . . . tacking . . . clipping the back in . . .
Testing for what's lacking.

Panasonic's manic anecdote is a cut-throat toilet float
Keeping conveyor topped up
System pristine and glistening
Yelling 'Mission Target Missing'
We're pissing in the wind if we wind up our cross hostile boss
A feminist lost the plot
Wants the most, we work like ghosts
Bodies no hosts.

But workers unite, fight
Take action seek a job satisfaction and a sanction
Against the mountains of the aforementioned mobile matter
Which gets fatter as we're sat there
Stacking . . . tacking . . . clipping the back in
Testing for what's lacking.
I'm not hacking it; in fact I'm hating it
Waiting for the long awaited weekend pay check
And Monday next you'll be perplexed
Cause I'm no fixed team member remember.

Jo Mapepe

OBLIVION

Winds of a thousand centuries
Endlessly sweeping
In a void of transparent darkness.

Come dry winds of times past
Sweep over me - swirl around me
And let your ageless arms
Of cool consolation enfold me
Within your deep peace.
Let your hands of remote stillness
My quivering nerves slowly numb,
Touch my parched, thirsting lips
With your pure breath of calmness,
And on your shoulders of nothing softness
Solace this desolate being.

Drift me away -
Away on a stream of stars
Through nights shadowed whispers
To merge with the purple dust.

D Holden

THE RAIN DANCE

The spirit lived within her, like a flame scorching her life.
He tried to cut it out, like a surgeon with a knife.
He watched in awe, with crystal eyes, never knowing what he'd find
Still the spirit burnt relentlessly, demanding fuel from her mind.

Then he performed a rain dance, as a last resort,
The raindrops drenched the flame and he found what he had sought,
A rainbow of apparent love, encircling the two,
Yet another saw a spark there and wondered what to do.

The spark flared once again and began to scorch her life,
He tried to cut it out, like a surgeon with a knife.
Pre-destined she flew away, a firefly out of sight,
To a moth, without a flame and to death, that dark-wet night.

The flame, his restless spirit, still scorching her strange life
Demanded still more fuel from his lost, unmarried wife,
Until her death became his death and they shimmered in the blaze,
Protected from the rain dance by a zephyr-like blue haze.

Christine Karalius

A LITTLE BOY'S LAMENT

Hey Father Christmas up there in your sleigh,
Did you get my letter I sent the other day?
I did not ask for a bicycle, a teddy bear or toys,
I did not ask for all the things you give to girls and boys.
So hey Father Christmas I hope you got my note,
I saw my mummy crying as I sat down and wrote,
I know her heart is breaking, there's nothing I can do,
I'm just a lonely, little boy, and so I'm asking you:
I just want you to bring my daddy back,
He went away a long, long time ago.
I'm hoping that you've got him in your sack,
'Cos Mummy says she really loves him so.
So please Father Christmas please bring back my dad,
As it will make my mummy so very, very glad,
So please Father Christmas just leave him by my bed,
And he might have a long, white beard and maybe dressed in red.
Dear Father Christmas could you be my dad.

Doris A Ballard

A LETTER IN VERSE

For a hundred thousand quid a year
and everything practically free,
I am your man, your link with the Top
if only you vote for me.
I don't like working as the masses do,
I want a job with no strain -
where I don't get sweaty and dirty
except in my scheming brain.
I won't have a toy boy or bimbo, not yet
I will wait and spy out the land
and see who wants a favour from me
and how much is put in my hand.
Honest and True, I care for you.
After me, you come first every time,
and that, to me, is a betrayal
of a career in Political crime.
Blue Tory, Yellow Lib, Red Labour PC,
Mostly brothers, as close as can be
of the same mould and think just the same -
how much can we make is the name of the game.

W S Booth

EXCUSE NUMBER ONE

I think I tried
Or did the most
With what I was given
I used it well
What can I say?
That gift from God
But waste is wasted.
I needed more
Than more could bring
But an empty vessel
Can never be filled.
The time has gone
Now a camel lies flat
I carry the straw
Which broke it's back
So I've nothing to lose now
The truth is I lied
It was all too much
So I never really tried.

Liam Allan

CONVERSATION WITH GOD

Life? Huh, I sat and said,
What kind of life was this.
A joke of a job, little money, poor self esteem.
Yeah, there must be a God alright.
He must be having a right good laugh at my expense.

I can't remember how it happened,
How my conversation with God began.
Books and people began to come my way,
Speaking of love and truth and hope.

And I began to realise that I had been asking
God to fix my life, my broken life, whilst
handing him very poor tools - fear,
doubt and despair.

As soon as I stopped spiting God and made
the time to listen, I was shown the way.
I was to 'be' love. 'Speak' truth. 'Live' hope.

It became apparent that I was more powerful
in thought, word and action than I had previously thought.
If I was to be a success in life - it was going
to have to be a 50:50 team effort.

Since this realisation, I have been lifted higher in every possible way,
If it can happen to me. Believe me, it can happen to you.
Just take a moment to talk with God . . .
And let him begin a conversation with you.
Do it now.

Kristine Morton

GOD

If I had the chance, there's many things,
That I would want to ask you,
Cos the world has all gone crazy,
Could we not start anew?
There's so many evil people,
Surely this was not your aim,
Hitler had a bad childhood!
Well, this is what they claim!
And so many people ask me,
What my theory is on you
And truthfully there's so much more,
That I feel you could do.

Cos to create this world, then you must be,
A man with so much power,
Much more so, than any human,
Whose greatest creation, was a concrete tower.

So tell me then, why you don't help,
Our world that's all gone wrong,
'Cause the cruelty of rape and murder,
Has been going on so long!
Now people fear each other,
There's no joining of our hands
And anger, pain and greed
Now sweep across our land.
And you must look upon us,
I wonder what you make of this,
I think you may feel sorrow
As this must not have been your wish!

So I ask you God with all my heart,
To make these people sane,
Grant us some hope and help us find,
A peaceful world again.

Catherine Perks

158

WEATHER

Lots of rainy days it seems to be,
pouring down it seems to me;
Hitting rooftops, bouncing off pavements,
reflecting shiny images as they went.

Frosty days are coming soon,
gales and gusts, some snow too,
icy hail and hair on end,
black ice, sharp and twisty bends.

Wendy Harrison

THE INSPIRATION OF SORROW

I lie quite alone, quite still
my heart pounds softly;
the tears are fathomless
but rise slowly, nearly -
soon to reach the overflow of life.
My longing lingers round every corner
and is left undesired.
My hoping hovers at the window
but is left unbroken.
Despair overrides humiliation
but irrational hopes prevail.
Love wails like the wind,
the soft rain moistens my pavements
quenching them with my falling tears.

Tamsin Heseltine

UNTITLED

Dear Mr Postman you are not to know
But Mr Bishop left this address
He left some time ago.

He was posted to another place
The Sorting Office in the sky
And I am wondering why
I still receive his mail.

Could it be the post-box
Which before its sad demise
Clearly stated on it, Mr Bishop died
Now I'm not blaming you Mr Postman
For doing a good job
It's just that Mr Bishop left
His name on every known mailing list
On several planets.

How can I prevent this man from becoming an immortal,
Who will be receiving offers to get rich
Or offers to borrow money to get rich
Long after I have gone?

Computer Banks around the world
Insist he is alive
And in a funny way of course they're right
Consistently my shadow receives
Far more mail than I
And worse, he gets more phone calls every night.

Dear Mr Postman I have a cunning plan
More cunning than a plan should ever be
I'll change my name to Bishop
Immortalise the man -
At least I'll know the mail is just for me.

Michael Price

ONE

One P45
One situation to survive
One big row at home
One fuse is blown
One life in a state
One love turns to hate
One wife battered and bruised
One kid kicked and abused
One more instant choice to make
One family to break
One kid in the middle
One dole cheque to fiddle
One kid runs to hide
One wife's suicide
One man on his own
One conscience to be shown
One patience has lapsed
One temper has snapped
One man stalks the street
One violence on heat
One broad on a bench
One false vengeance to quench
One glare in the eye
One pair of hands to be tied
One gun to her heart
One pair of legs forced apart
One horrible pain
One cry out in vain
One mouth to be taped
One female brutally raped
'I'm so sorry' he said
As he blew off his own head.

Alan Groves

MOTHER'S DAY

On this your special Mother's Day, I think of you,
I give thanks to the Lord
For I had not one mother but two.
So different in your ways
But with so much love in your hearts,
With that special gift
You could not tell you apart.
One is in heaven now,
So by her photo I leave a rose,
The other I send this little verse,
All the love I send with it
- only she knows.

P Richardson

FRIENDSHIP

Friendship is a road,
One day it will be silky smooth,
The next will be rugged rough,
It will be a wide friendship, or a
Country lane friendship,
It may be worn away or brand new,
Most are everlasting,
But some are cul-de-sacs.

Francesca Stubbins (12)

FOREVER

Victoria, Emma, Mel B and C,
Had a No 1 Hit with 'Wannabe'.
Way back then in '96,
Of course they were sure to release a mix.

Then in '97 they sacked Simon Fuller,
Geri and Mel to become their ruler,
Also in '97 the movie came out,
It shot to No 1 without a doubt.

No reason for departure did Geri give,
No matter what 'The Spice Girls' live,
Rumours of a break-up between the tour,
Nothing could stop 'em - they began as four!

Expectant mothers - Victoria and Mel B,
Spice babies - Brooklyn and Phoenix Chi,
Independence Day - Victoria's wedding joy,
Happy as could be with 'David' - her spice boy.

Mel B's wedding breaks on New Year's Day,
Quietly recovered on a foreign holiday,
Mel C and Geri - share a stage,
Victoria - the cause of a health outrage!

We hope they continue for many a year,
Releasing pop music to flow in the ear,
What will Spice Generation bring?
Let's find out . . . summary in the spring.

Barry Shaw

OUR TREE

I want to take you new and find, I want to plant us by the sea
A bank where a rushing river lie with no one but you and me
But below the arched, creaking back, I watch it climb the sky
Our internal reaching, twisting tree that still grows inside my mind.

On this huge, green tree growing to black, I carve two names into wood
Here I sit; you've dowsed its flames
Over there, leaving here, with your back to me;
A new seed dropped and growing fast
Shading me from the warm summer's sun.

My blowing strength, my cracking hopes
Opens your mind but you don't edge close
You turn away, closing your eyes, holding your tears,
                                        gripping your pride
A long branch stretched but held on tight
And gripped back right by nails in your feet.

You hammer in fast and set your ground
Ten stubborn roots, one for each toe
Your soul wants to move to mix with mine
Why won't you knot with my branches now?

I try to fuse, tie your love to me
But the more I try, the more it withers, the more it dies,
                                        the less it climbs
I watch your face as it grows older
Forced from mine, over my shoulder.

The fire in our tree has disappeared and gone
You're separate now, with no thought at all
I sit within, wishing return
Of your match, a spark or two stone flints
But the old tree rots and down it falls
My new seed forced to blow away
And settle parted away from yours
In places in which we'll stay.

Joe Reese (16)

RAIN POEM

Rain is coming down
Making lots of puddles
For me to jump, play
And splash in.

Rain is making floods
Across all the fields
I can see the birds
Using them as baths.

Rain is coming down
In big, hard drops
Landing on the roofs
With a big splish-splosh.

Daniel Sloan (8)

THE BLAZING STAR

The Sun is an egg
Sizzling in the sky,
The Sun is an orange
Trying to fly.
The Sun is a star
Shimmering in space,
The Sun is a face
Having grace.
The Sun is Saturn
Bouncing out of its ring,
The Sun is a melon
About to sing.
The Sun is as spherical
As a bouncing ball,
The Sun is a ball
About to fall.
The Sun is a tiger
Waiting to roar,
The Sun is our future!

Miranda McCabe (10)

HUGS

It's wonders what a hug can do,
A hug can cheer you when you're blue.
A hug can say, 'I love you so' or 'Hey I
hate to see you go'.
Hugs are great for fathers and mothers
Sweet for sisters, cool for brothers.
And chances are some favourite aunts
Love them more than potted plants
So stretch those arms without delay
And give someone a *hug today.*

Stephanie Amanda Holt (13)

MY LOVE

A spring morning, an autumn day,
A summer afternoon where everything's gay.
All year round I'm forced to say
'My love.'

In the great year of '53.
Sat by the table with a cup of tea
A young lad proposed to me.
My love.

In '54 he married me.
We sat on a swing made on a tree,
It was so romantic to me.
My love.

All year round he says to me
With milk, coffee or herbal tea,
'I really love thee. You are truly
My love.'

Damien Jones (12)

GO TO BED!

Go to bed!
Mum, I need to be fed
Now go to bed!
You forgot to give me my bread
Now go to bed!
You forgot to put the baby to bed and it needs to be fed
Go to bed!
You said I could stay up to 11pm today
After all that moaning now it's time for school
Go to school!
You forgot to give me my tool
Now go to school!
School's over, it's midnight
Go to bed!
You forgot all this moaning, it's the summer holidays
Just go to bed!

Faye Taylor (10)

THE DEVIL RIDES IN

The Devil rides in on the strike of a clock,
His black mantle covers the earth.

The ground opens up with a triumphant crack,
Erupting its terrible birth.

The Grim Reaper smiles at his blackened deed,
From the ground climbs up like an evil seed.

White bone and black hearts dance and depart,
Back and forth to the Devil's tune.
What joy rotting corpses have in a frenzy,
Watched by the watery moon.

But hark! A cock crows, revelry halts,
And death's smile slips.
He points to the sky as dawn draws close by,
No words form on his bony lips.

As the Devil rides out,
The sun rises up and lights up in the world
Once more.
But under the earth the dead wait in silence for
The Devil to open the door.

Dulcie Metcalfe (11)

NO FUEL!

The petrol has run out
Mr Blair has had a shout
Will all you tankers please pull out
Go and fill our garages about
But I don't mind 'cos I'll walk to school
'Cos I don't need *no fuel!*
'Cos I've got energy and I'm healthy too
'Cos I exercise all year through.

Steven Kennedy (12)

I'D LIKE TO BE AN ACTOR WITH DOMINIC WOOD

I've always wanted to be a star
That's my dream come true,
My mates would always say to me
One day it could be you.
But I've got to do my GCSEs
And be brainy as I could
Then I'd have to write to some people
And have an interview.
Then I would be a star
And get with Dominic Wood
I'd take him back to my place
And cook some romantic food.
I think he is a total babe
And I want to do a show like he does
With the fantastic Dominic Wood.
I'd want to become a star
That's my dream come true
I'd look in the mirror and say
One day it could be you!

Natasha Kington

A POEM ABOUT ASTRO!

A cuddly bear that feels like sponge,
Triangular nose and a great big smile,
Ears are shaped as a semicircle
And lovely, dotty, black eyes
Round his neck he has a blue-jean collar
Astro is grey and his little tail is grey too.
That is Astro!

Eleanor Whyte (9)

I WISH I WASN'T A WESTLIFE FAN!

I wish I wasn't a Westlife fan,
Because they are so naff.
I wish there was a Westlife ban,
Then I wouldn't look so daft.

Why can't I like limp biscuit more,
They are much more butch.
I wish I wasn't a Westlife bore,
And I'd be one of the 'dudes'!

I wish Westlife would split up now,
And rescue me from myself.
Westlife singing is worse than a cow,
Why can't I leave them on my shelf?

Tony Callaghan (14)

I DIDN'T GET TICKETS

I didn't get tickets,
To go and see Westlife.
I didn't get tickets,
I was really let down.
I didn't get tickets,
It's left me in such a strife.
I didn't get tickets,
It gave me such a frown.

Stephanie Clark (18)

ME, MY MOBILE AND I

I'm addicted 2 my mobile
We're never far apart
If u c me without it
I've got a broken heart.

If I dunot have my mobile
It makes me v-sad
And I get all x-cited
When I pick up 2 my dad.

Kathleen Prescott (17)

LYING ON THE SHORE

Lying on the shore,
In the midday sun.
I listen to the waves,
Watch water glisten in the sun.

I think it is relaxing,
The sound of the waves crashing.
The way the seagulls call,
They make me feel so small.

Flying through the air,
In the sun's full glare.
They swoop and glide in the air,
As I'm lying on the shore.

Colin Clarke (14)

AND THEN YOU WENT

Please don't say her name,
Now she's gone away.
You can't understand the pain,
When that one word you say.

Her voice is like a summer's day,
I'm so sad I'll never hear it again.
Her laughter is like the sun's hot rays,
Now it's gone, tears fall like rain.

As my heart bleeds it leaves a stain,
My heart is a tall ship, locked in your bay.
First you came,
Then you went away;

And you took my heart with you.

Brian Ford (15)

HOMEWORK O HOMEWORK

Homework, O homework
I hate you, you stink
I wish I could wash you away in the sink.
If only a bomb would explode you to bits
Homework, O homework
I hate you, you stink.

I'd rather take a bath with a man-eating shark
Or wrestle a lion alone in the dark
Eat spinach and liver, pet ten porcupine
Than tackling the homework my teacher makes.

Homework, O homework
You're last on my list
I simply can't see why you even exist
If you would just disappear it would tickle me pink
Homework, O homework
I hate you, you stink.

Emma Garland (8)

WINTER

Short days, long nights, telly in the evening
Leaves falling off trees, crunch, crunch, crunch
Icy path slipping over skid, skid, skid
Short days, long nights, telly in the evening
Some snow white, white snow
Some fog thick, thick fog
Short days, long nights, telly in the evening
It's winter!

Grace Whyte (10)

THE SPIDER PLANT

The leaves resembled spiders legs
Long, thin and bent,
Dull green, staring, tangled hair,
Like a witch's curved nail stopping.
Rattling in the vulgar, wild wind,
Razor-keen edges slashing,
Rats clamber far into the ground,
Like worms swarming sharply,
Like volcanoes spitting its earth,
Destroying venom sending out its
Poisonous clouds!

Georgia Leckie (10)

A POEM

The eagle swift, the eagle fast,
Flies above the great ship's mast.
The wooden mast, it stands proud,
Hears the cry of the seagulls loud.
The seagulls white, the seagulls gay,
Swooping past the sheltered bay.

Rachel Ann Fletcher (8)

ROUTINE

Routine is good,
routine is bad,
With routine you'll never feel sad.

Wake up in the morning,
Have a quick wash,
Go to school acting posh.

School is finished,
Homework to do,
Rushed home for the loo.

Now I'm home,
Arrived home late,
My dinner's on my plate.

Done my homework,
Off to bed
Before my mum even said.

Wake up in the morning,
Rushing all about,
Screams and shouts.

Routine is good,
routine is bad,
With routine you'll never feel sad.

Kimberley Davies (11)

I Am The Wind

I turn your umbrellas inside out,
I make you catch a cold,
I make your house fall down,
If I'm really angry and cold.
I scare you in bed,
I bang on your window,
When it is hot I blow on your face.
I blow out your candles and fires,
When you are not looking.

Beware of me!

Fay Whyte (12)

ENCOUNTER WITH A FORGOTTEN SELF

As I walk down the burning amber road,
I trace the footsteps before me,
Where sandalled feet have trod
And run and jumped and skipped their way,
To where stones melt into sand
And ragged robins grace the dunes.

A kind of tenderness comes over me
When I step over crumbling fortresses,
Feeling grains between my toes.
I see her now, this child of antiquity.
Her head of ribbons and jasper eyes
Ignites a spark of recognition,
A flickering resemblance
To a distant memory.

She fades into shadow and is gone,
Locked in a gilded moment forever,
where dreams and memories collide.
The salty breeze carries away
The echoes of laughter
And I turn and continue walking in the footsteps of
ghosts.

Laura Smith

MY DAD

My dad's a fireman,
Brave and bold,
He puts out the flames
When they take hold.
He reminds me of
The knights of old.
He rescues people in distress
From their smoky wilderness.
He went into a house
Where there were children three
And got an award for bravery.
I would not change my dad,
Not me.

Chloe Wooldridge (14)

Don't Make Me Think

I don't like it
When people make me think.
It makes me
Grumpy, bumpy:
It's driving me to drink!

Don't mention Peter Andre,
It makes me really sad.
I used to like him when
My taste was:
Really, *really*, bad!

Don't make me end,
This poem.

Caroline Dawson

MY PAPA

I really like my papa,
That's my mother's dad.
Right now, he is really ill
And that makes me very sad.

He smells a lot of lavender
And wears a dressing gown,
He used to do some exercise,
Now he just stays in bed.

He never liked doing gardening,
He watches TV instead,
And he eats a lot of chips
With tomato sauce!

Not brown sauce, red!

Shaun Teece

A DAY OF JUST ME AND DAD

I remember a day
When only me and my dad remained.
The sun shone,
It never rained.
We were swimming, dancing
Singing, glancing.
I am never, ever like a rogue,
My favourite singer is Kylie Minogue.
I really love going to the park,
It's really hard; this lace-tying lark.
I get really upset
When something happens to my loved dad,
But when he recovers,
I'm ever so glad.
The day I had with my loved and
Honourable dad
Was the best day I'd ever had.
My girlfriend Stephanie's such a honey,
I am raring to win lots of money!

James Agnew (15)

FOR VICKY

Softly heaven called you,
It whispered to you and you came.
You trod silently upwards
And passed us all unseen.

Your voice is now a soul,
Treading upon the wind,
Gently drying tears that fall
With a touch that cannot be pinned.

And every time the wind
Brushes against my cheek,
I know that it is by you that I
Have been softly kissed.

And though I miss you, terribly

And wish that you were near,
I see you in the star-filled night
And know that you are here.

You are present in the sunshine
And in the pleasant air,
I know that you are in my heart
And that is all I care.

I know one day I'll see you
As you were before,
For now the wind will have to do,
I cannot be with you more.

Christina Mallon

FOG

The fog came down the glen,
Creeping at first,
Then engulfing,
Settling, waiting, watching,
Waiting like death,
Like death waits for its prey.

The fog came slithering down the glen,
Encasing,
Encasing the glen in its richness.

The fog came tumbling down the glen,
Silent and gentle, until the day arises,
Transpires.

For it will happen again, and again,
The fog will come down the glen.

Neil Burns